W9-BLI-439

BIOMES OF THE EARTH

WETLANDS

Peter D. Moore

Illustrations by
Richard Garratt

CHELSEA HOUSE
PUBLISHERS
An imprint of Infobase Publishing

Wetlands

Copyright © 2006 by Peter D. Moore

All rights reserved. No part of this book may be reproduced or utilized in any form or by any means, electronic or mechanical, including photocopying, recording, or by any information storage or retrieval systems, without permission in writing from the publisher. For information contact:

Chelsea House
An imprint of Infobase Publishing
132 West 31st Street
New York NY 10001

Library of Congress Cataloging-in-Publication Data
Moore, Peter D.
Wetlands / Peter D. Moore ; illustrations by Richard Garratt.
    p. cm.—(Biomes of the Earth)
  Includes bibliographical references and index.
  ISBN 0-8160-5324-3
  1. Wetland ecology—Juvenile literature. 2. Wetlands—Juvenile literature. I. Garratt, Richard, ill. II. Title. III. Series.
  QH541.5.M3M664 2006
  577.68—dc22   2005009085

Chelsea House books are available at special discounts when purchased in bulk quantities for businesses, associations, institutions, or sales promotions. Please call our Special Sales Department in New York at (212) 967-8800 or (800) 322-8755.

You can find Chelsea House on the World Wide Web at http://www.chelseahouse.com

Text design by David Strelecky
Cover design by Cathy Rincon
Illustrations by Richard Garratt
Photo research by Elizabeth H. Oakes

Printed in China

CP Hermitage 10 9 8 7 6 5 4 3 2 1

This book is printed on acid-free paper.

From Peter Moore:
To Eunice, Helen, and Caroline

From Richard Garratt:
To Chantal, who has lightened my darkness

CONTENTS

PREFACE

Earth is a remarkable planet. There is nowhere else in our solar system where life can survive in such a great diversity of forms. As far as we can currently tell, our planet is unique. Isolated in the barren emptiness of space, here on Earth we are surrounded by a remarkable range of living things, from the bacteria that inhabit the soil to the great whales that migrate through the oceans, from the giant redwood trees of the Pacific forests to the mosses that grow on urban sidewalks. In a desolate universe, Earth teems with life in a bewildering variety of forms.

One of the most exciting things about the Earth is the rich pattern of plant and animal communities that exists over its surface. The hot, wet conditions of the equatorial regions support dense rain forests with tall canopies occupied by a wealth of animals, some of which may never touch the ground. The cold, bleak conditions of the polar regions, on the other hand, sustain a much lower variety of species of plants and animals, but those that do survive under such harsh conditions have remarkable adaptations to their testing environment. Between these two extremes lie many other types of complex communities, each well suited to the particular conditions of climate prevailing in its region. Scientists call these communities *biomes*.

The different biomes of the world have much in common with one another. Each has a plant component, which is responsible for trapping the energy of the Sun and making it available to the other members of the community. Each has grazing animals, both large and small, that take advantage of the store of energy found within the bodies of plants. Then come the predators, ranging from tiny spiders that feed upon even smaller insects to tigers, eagles, and polar bears that survive by preying upon large animals. All of these living things form a complicated network of feeding interactions, and, at the base of the system, microbes in the soil are ready to consume the energy-rich plant litter or dead animal flesh that remains. The biome, then, is an integrated unit within which each species plays its particular role.

This set of books aims to outline the main features of each of the Earth's major biomes. The biomes covered include the tundra habitats of polar regions and high mountains, the taiga (boreal forest) and temperate forests of somewhat warmer lands, the grasslands of the prairies and the tropical savanna, the deserts of the world's most arid locations, and the tropical forests of the equatorial regions. The wetlands of the world, together with river and lake habitats, do not lie neatly in climatic zones over the surface of the Earth but are scattered over the land. And the oceans are an exception to every rule. Massive in their extent, they form an interconnecting body of water extending down into unexplored depths, gently moved by global currents.

Humans have had an immense impact on the environment of the Earth over the past 10,000 years since the last Ice Age. There is no biome that remains unaffected by the presence of the human species. Indeed, we have created our own biome in the form of agricultural and urban lands, where people dwell in greatest densities. The farms and cities of the Earth have their own distinctive climates and natural history, so they can be regarded as a kind of artificial biome that people have created, and they are considered as a separate biome in this set.

Each biome is the subject of a separate volume. Each richly illustrated book describes the global distribution, the climate, the rocks and soils, the plants and animals, the history, and the environmental problems found within each biome. Together, the set provides students with a sound basis for understanding the wealth of the Earth's biodiversity, the factors that influence it, and the future dangers that face the planet and our species.

Is there any practical value in studying the biomes of the Earth? Perhaps the most compelling reason to understand the way in which biomes function is to enable us to conserve their rich biological resources. The world's productivity is the basis of the human food supply. The world's biodiversity holds a wealth of unknown treasures, sources of drugs and medicines that will help to improve the quality of life. Above all, the world's biomes are a constant source of wonder, excitement, recreation, and inspiration that feed not only our bodies but also our minds and spirits. These books aim to provide the information about biomes that readers need in order to understand their function, draw upon their resources, and, most of all, enjoy their diversity.

ACKNOWLEDGMENTS

I should like to record my gratitude to the editorial staff at Chelsea House for their untiring support, assistance, and encouragement during the preparation of this book. Frank K. Darmstadt, executive editor, has been a constant source of advice and information, and Dorothy Cummings, project editor, has edited the text with unerring skill and impeccable care. I am grateful to you both. I should also like to thank Richard Garratt for his excellent illustrations and Elizabeth Oakes for her perceptive selection of photographs. I have also greatly appreciated the help and guidance of Mike Allaby, my fellow author at Chelsea House. Thanks to my wife, who has displayed a remarkable degree of patience and support during the writing of this book, together with much-needed critical appraisal, and to my daughters, Helen and Caroline, who have supplied ideas and materials that have enriched the text. I must also acknowledge the contribution of many generations of students in the Life Sciences Department of the University of London, King's College, who have been a constant source of stimulation and who will recall (I trust) many of the ideas contained here. Thanks are also due to my colleagues in teaching and research, especially those who have accompanied me on field courses and research visits to many parts of the world. Their work underlies the science presented in this book.

INTRODUCTION

Wetlands may not have the grandeur of towering mountain ranges, but they still rank among the most spectacular and impressive of the Earth's ecosystems. When observed through banks of reeds into the open waters of a lake or witnessed from the edge of a treeless bog in the lands of the far north, wetlands can evoke a sense of wilderness that few other ecosystems can achieve. One can imagine how the Victorian explorer John Speke must have felt when he emerged from the endless savanna plains of East Africa and saw for the first time the immense swamps and marshes that surround the enormous extent of Lake Victoria. It is a water body far too wide to see the opposite shore, bounded by rich marshes of papyrus in which hippopotamuses wallow and flocks of waterfowl feed. Speke recorded his great excitement at being the first European to view this fabled wetland that had cost him time, effort, and health to reach. It was probably the greatest moment of his life.

Visitors to the wetlands today can capture that same spirit of discovery and adventure. Their wildness is exciting, but it has led some to dismiss wetlands as worthless wet deserts. This is far from the truth because wetlands are a rich source of biodiversity, containing large numbers of plants and animals that can exist in no other habitat. They also supply the needs of many of the world's people. All people need water, and wetlands provide the obvious natural reservoir that we should conserve with care. This is the message of this book.

What are wetlands?

The term *wetland* may seem an easy one to understand; it is a region of the world that is wet. But actually defining a wetland is more difficult than one might expect. Tropical rain forests are wet, but they are not strictly wetlands. The wetland biome includes all regions where shallow water, either fresh or salty, stands or moves over the surface of the land. The oceans, seas, and deep lakes are normally excluded from the definition of a wetland, but the shallow edges of lakes and seas are regarded as wetlands. In order to make the definition of wetland more precise, delegates from many countries met in Ramsar, Iran, in 1971. The resulting international agreement, known as the Ramsar Convention, defines wetlands as "all areas of marsh, fen, peat land, or water, whether natural or artificial, permanent or temporary, with water that is static or flowing, fresh, brackish, or salt." It sets a depth of 20 feet (6 m) as the limit for an area of water to fall within the definition of a wetland.

Unlike most biomes, which are restricted to certain climatic zones of the Earth, wetlands are found throughout the world. They are, however, more common in some parts of the world than in others, as we shall see. In total they occupy around 6 percent of the Earth's surface. Because they are found in so many different climatic situations, they take a very wide range of forms. The wetlands of the Arctic are very different from those found near the equator, in the hot, wet Tropics. The wetlands of central Australia are very different from those of southern Florida. This book examines these differences and consider how the different climates, soils, and topography affect the shape, size, and structure of the different wetland types. It also explores how the wetlands change over time as the plants and animals that inhabit them cause the wetlands to develop in predictable ways. Wetlands are always changing, and people need to understand the causes and the direction of these changes to be able to conserve, protect, and care for this fragile habitat.

Some of the diversity found in wetlands results from the chemistry of the waters that drain into them. This, in turn, is closely related to the geology of the rocks that underlie them and form the watersheds in which the wetlands lie. Chemistry and geology influence the composition of the communities of plants and animals that occupy wetlands. Some of these organisms are extremely demanding in their requirements, surviving only where certain chemical elements are in rich supply. The geology of a catchment also provides the eroded fragments of rock that weather down to small particles and accumulate in wetlands as sediment. The buildup of sediments in wetlands is one of the factors that leads to the changes that constantly occur, as water becomes shallower and the vegetation alters accordingly. The sediments also record the changes that take place. In the course of time the silts and muds of wetlands form layers that may remain undisturbed for thousands of years. By boring into these layers, scientists can discover a great deal about the history of the development of the wetland and even find evidence of changes in the whole landscape and the prevailing climate of the past. Wetland sediments are an archive of past events, lying beneath the surface and waiting to be read.

A wetland develops over time out of the interaction between the living components of the habitat (the plants and animals) and the nonliving components (water, chemicals, and rock particles). Together, the living and nonliving elements thus form an integrated ecosystem. The living organisms also interact with one another: Plants provide food for grazers; grazers are eaten by predators; and these in turn are consumed by larger predators. All excrete materials from their bodies, and those that are not eaten die and become food for detritivores, the animals that feed upon dead materials, or to the bacteria and fungi that finally consume any remaining detritus. Energy flows through this ecosystem from one level to another, and materials circulate around the system and are reused and conserved within it. Understanding these ecosystem functions is key to managing the ecosystem sensitively without destroying it in the process. It also makes it possible to safely remove useful materials from the wetland, for example, fish for human consumption or reeds for making roofs.

Water is essential to all life, and the abundant supply of water in the wetlands makes them a very productive ecosystem. An excess of water, on the other hand, can bring certain problems to living creatures, both plants and animals. All organisms also need oxygen, but living in water can bring problems in this respect. Although oxygen dissolves in water, it travels much more slowly in this medium than in air and can be in short supply, especially if the water is stagnant. So wetland plants and animals need special adaptations to cope with these conditions. This book looks at how the wetland species manage to deal with the many problems that confront them and how the great range of wetland types in the world has led to the development of a high level of biodiversity.

Why are wetlands important?

Wetlands have existed on Earth for hundreds of millions of years. Some of the wetlands of ancient times, such as the coal-forming swamps that predate the dinosaurs, are of enormous economic importance today. Without the formation of coal, the industrial revolution and our current industrial society would never have developed. Our present way of life is, in a sense, a consequence of the existence of wetlands in the past and the energy stored up in the geological deposits they formed. When humans first appeared on Earth, they learned to live in wetlands and to use their resources, taking fish from their waters, trapping birds, burning peat, and draining the edges for agriculture. In some parts of the world whole villages were erected on stilts so that the people could live close to the water and yet be safe from floods. Even today there are peoples, such as the Marsh Arabs of southern Iraq, whose way of life depends on wetlands. To some extent all people rely on wetlands as the source of water for drinking, hygiene, and agricultural irrigation. The world's living wetlands continue to be used as a source of peat, which serves as both a source of energy and a soil additive in gardens. (Peat extraction, however, is a major threat to wetland survival and a use of peat lands that is not sustainable.) A proportion of the waste carbon dioxide that human activities inject into the atmosphere by burning coal and oil is absorbed by the growth of peat in wetlands, which thus help clean the atmosphere of human-caused pollution. *Wetlands* will examine the ways people benefit from wetlands and look at how we can conserve them and the rich assemblage of life they contain.

As world populations continue to grow and people demand more in the way of the Earth's resources, it is important to look closely at the natural biomes of the world that are, after all, our support system. Biomes of the Earth is a set of books aimed at encouraging an interest in and a concern for the natural world and an appreciation of the part that humans must play in managing the planet. Here we look at one of the world's most threatened ecosystems, the wetland.

CHAPTER 1

GEOGRAPHY OF WETLANDS

The water cycle

One thing that all wetlands have in common is an abundance of water. Water is a remarkable material in many ways. It is one of few compounds that exist as a gas, a liquid, and a solid (ice) within the range of temperatures that Earth regularly experiences. Except on high mountains or in the polar regions, water is most often seen in its liquid state, which is found between 32°F and 212°F (0°C and 100°C). Above its boiling point liquid water is totally converted into vapor, but even at lower temperatures some water is found in this form. The air that people breathe contains water vapor, and when expelled it is enriched in water vapor from their moist lungs. Water enters the atmosphere not only from the evaporation that takes place in people's lungs but also from all water surfaces, including the surfaces of the oceans, lakes, rivers, streams, vegetation, and soils. Vegetation produces relatively large quantities of water vapor compared with bare soil. This is because leaf surfaces are covered with tiny pores called *stomata,* through which they take in the gas carbon dioxide from the atmosphere as they photosynthesize. In the course of absorbing this gas, the leaf pores lose water vapor in a process called *transpiration.* All land and water surfaces, therefore, are supplying water vapor to the atmosphere through evaporation or transpiration. The combination of these two sources of water vapor is called *evapotranspiration.*

Warm air can contain more water vapor than cool air, and when air cools—as, for example, when it is pushed by wind up the sides of mountains—it is able to hold less water vapor. Consequently, the water condenses as droplets, forming cloud. If these drops become large, they fall as rain. If the air temperature drops below the freezing point of water, then water droplets become crystals of ice and fall in the form of snowflakes. Water falling from the atmosphere as either rain-drops or snow is termed *precipitation*. When snow falls in situations that are permanently cold, such as over polar ice caps or very high mountains, it becomes compacted into ice that may remain in that form for long periods of time. But rainfall and melting ice supply the land with liquid water that follows the pull of gravity, cascading over rocks in mountain streams, soaking into the soil and draining through porous rocks, or moving gently through the wetlands on its way to the ocean. Water is almost always on the move, and its global movement is known as the *hydrological cycle*.

The hydrological cycle is shown in the illustration. From this diagram we can see that 97 percent of the world's surface water is contained in the oceans and is saline, or salty. Of the remaining 3 percent, which consists of freshwater, 2.25 percent is locked up in the ice caps and glaciers of the world. The remaining 0.75 percent is actually moving through the soils and the wetlands of the Earth's land surface. Although this may seem a very small proportion of the world's total water resources, it is an extremely important component of the water cycle. It supports all of the plants and animals that live upon the surface of the land, each of which needs a daily intake of this vital material. Meanwhile, the water falling from the skies is replaced by evaporation, largely from the oceans. About 84 percent of the total input of water vapor to the atmosphere comes from the oceans, the remainder being supplied by evapotranspiration from the land surface, including vegetation, lakes, and wetlands.

The constant movement of water over the land surface as it returns to the ocean has a strong influence on the development of landscapes, eroding the materials in its path and creating river valleys and canyons in the process. Chemical elements are dissolved from the rocks and soils though which water passes and are carried to the sea. But these elements are largely left behind when water evaporates once more, so the seas become increasingly rich in salts and other chemicals. (The chemistry of waters and wetlands will be discussed in chapter 2.) On the whole, wetlands in inland locations tend to have low concentrations of elements (although there are some important exceptions) because the water is

ice 2.25% freshwater 0.75% saltwater oceans 97%

P precipitation
E evaporation
E/T evapotranspiration

constantly moving through them, so chemicals do not accumulate there. But lakes, swamps, and peat lands slow down the passage of water from sky to sea, reducing the erosive effect of the moving water and also acting as temporary storage reservoirs.

The global hydrological cycle. The figures indicate what proportion of the world's water is present as ice, freshwater, and salt water.

Where on Earth are the wetlands?

Wetlands may form anywhere there is a reliable source of precipitation or drainage water. Unlike many of the other biomes, such as tropical rain forest, savanna, desert, temperate forest, or tundra, which are restricted to distinct climatic zones of the Earth's land surface, wetlands are not limited in this way. Away from the coastal regions, which have a permanent supply of water, wetlands tend to be most abundant where precipitation is abundant. The map on page 4 shows the regions of the world where wetlands are more commonly found, and it can be seen that their greatest concentration occurs in two main regions. One is the Tropics, and the other is in the cool temperate zone of northern Asia, Europe, and North America. Both of these regions, especially the Tropics, have high rainfall, and the generally cool temperatures of the northern regions means that rates of evaporation and transpiration are lower, so more water remains in the soils.

The map also shows that wetlands are far more abundant in the Northern Hemisphere than in the Southern Hemisphere. The Northern Hemisphere wetlands are largely located between latitudes 45°N and 75°N; the Southern Hemisphere contains very little land in the equivalent latitudes. The southern island of New Zealand and the southern

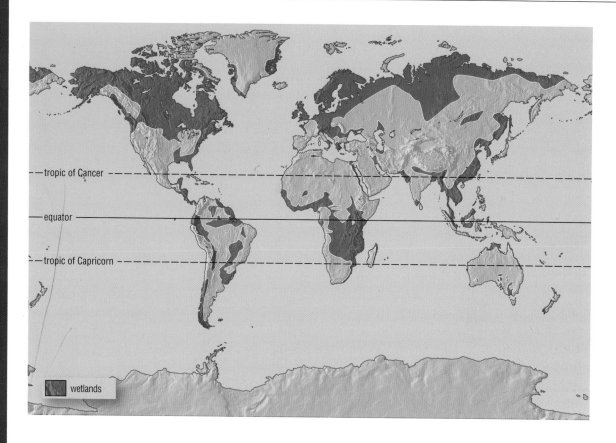

The distribution of wetlands through the world

tip of South America, together with some other small islands, such as the Falkland Islands, contain the only land within these latitudes in the Southern Hemisphere, and these regions are rich in wetlands.

The explanation for these two bands of wetlands, in the Tropics and the cool temperate regions, is to be found in the pattern of energy distribution and atmospheric circulation over the surface of the Earth. The illustration shows the way in which solar energy reaches different parts of the globe. The solar radiation reaching the equatorial regions arrives from a Sun that is almost directly overhead at noon for much of the year. The light that falls vertically passes through less thickness of atmosphere than in the temperate regions, and more energy reaches the land surface. The higher latitudes (that is, those closer to the poles) receive energy from the Sun at a lower angle, so that energy is spread over a wider region than at the equator, and the light has traveled through a greater depth of atmosphere, so more energy has been absorbed (see the illustration). The consequence of these differences in radiant energy is that the equatorial regions become warmer than the temperate zone. The warm, moist air of the Tropics is forced upward by denser, cooler air moving toward the equator. When air rises, it cools. For every 1,000 feet we rise above the surface of the Earth, the air temperature drops by about 3.6°F (equivalent to 6.5°C for each 1,000 meters in height). As has been described, cooler air is able to hold less water vapor than warm air, so water droplets condense in the rising air and fall as torrential rain in the equatorial zone. The abundance of rain produced in this way ensures that wetlands are abundant in this equatorial region.

The cool air produced at high altitude is pushed away from the equator, and, since cool air is denser than warm air, it starts to sink once more. Between latitudes 20° and 30° (north and south of the equator) this cool, dry air sinks and produces a zone of the Earth that is characterized by an arid climate. These belts of land in the Northern and Southern Hemispheres are where the deserts are mainly found, and wetlands are scarce. The wetlands that are present are either coastal in distribution or may be formed for short periods of time and then lost because of heat and drought, as is the case

Distribution of solar energy over the surface of the Earth

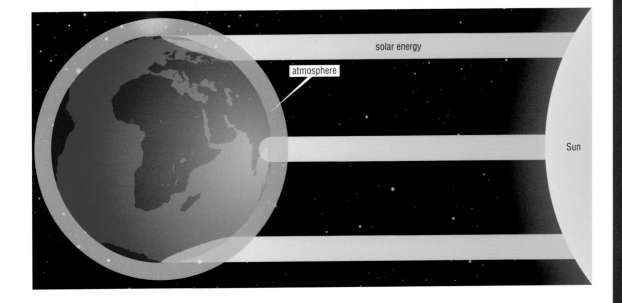

in central Australia. The dense, descending air in these latitudes spreads out toward both the equator and the poles. The poleward-moving mass of air that has been warmed by its contact with the hot desert lands eventually collides with masses of cold, dense air from the poles, headed toward the equator. This collision forces the warmer air, which has picked up moisture in its journey poleward, upward as the denser polar air mass pushes beneath it, and the result is great atmospheric instability. Precipitation is high in this unstable region (between latitudes 50° and 70°), falling as rain in summer and snow in winter. Within this cool temperate, wet zone wetlands are once more very abundant (see the map on page 4).

The general pattern of wetland zones seen in the map can therefore be explained by the global pattern of precipitation resulting from the uneven heating of the Earth's surface and the consequent atmospheric movements. There are, however, complications found within this general picture. In India, for example, which is north of the equator but within the Tropics, the summer brings the hot zone of rising air closer, and rainfall increases in the form of torrential rain, known as the *monsoon*. These rains are prevented from moving farther north into Asia by the high mountains of the Himalayas, which form a chain along the northern edge of the Indian subcontinent, and the precipitation trapped by the mountains floods back into India, Pakistan, and Bangladesh, leading to the development of wetlands in the low-lying regions of these countries. To the north, beyond the Himalayas, the rain-bearing air masses fail to penetrate, and desert conditions prevail. Here, in the Gobi Desert, wetlands are almost nonexistent.

Ocean currents also affect global patterns of precipitation and therefore the distribution of wetlands. A warm oceanic current (the North Pacific Drift) moves east across the Pacific Ocean and arrives at the west coast of North America in Oregon and Washington states, passing north along the coast of British Columbia in Canada. The warm, moist air produced by this current brings abundant rain to this coastline, resulting in the development of temperate rain forests and an abundance of wetlands. There is a similar warm current (the

Gulf Stream) that moves east through the North Atlantic Ocean, taking water from the Caribbean Sea to the western parts of northern Europe and leading to high precipitation and a widespread development of wetlands in these regions.

Hence the combined global effects of solar energy input, air mass movements, and the effect of high mountains and oceanic currents explain the general pattern of wetland distribution over the face of the Earth. But what controls the precise location of wetlands within the landscape of these regions? To understand this, we must consider the patterns of wetlands and their controlling factors at the landscape scale rather than the global scale.

Wetland distribution in the landscape

If asked to suggest where they would expect to find wetlands in a particular landscape, most people would probably say in the valleys or lowlands rather than up on the mountaintops or on the slopes. In general, this is entirely correct. Water moves downhill under the influence of gravity, and it moves fastest where the slopes are steepest, so it is down in the low-lying regions of valleys and floodplains that wetlands are likely to be most commonly found.

Not only does water move more slowly as the slope becomes less steep, but it accumulates in the valleys as it is gathered in from the surrounding regions. One can think of the hills and the slopes as the ground from which water is collected and the valley floors as the receiving areas. The collecting ground for water is called the *catchment* or the *watershed* of a valley. The area of the watershed in relation to that of the receiving area of the valley floor has an important effect on how much water moves into the valley. For example, suppose that for every square foot (900 sq cm) of valley floor there are 10 square feet (.9 sq m) of surrounding slopes in the watershed. If, during a storm, one inch (2.54 cm) of rain falls over the catchment, and if all this water moves down into the valley floor, then this receiving region would have the equivalent of 10 inches (25.4 cm) of rain. Whether or not a wetland would form in such a valley depends on whether some or all of this water is retained there or instead

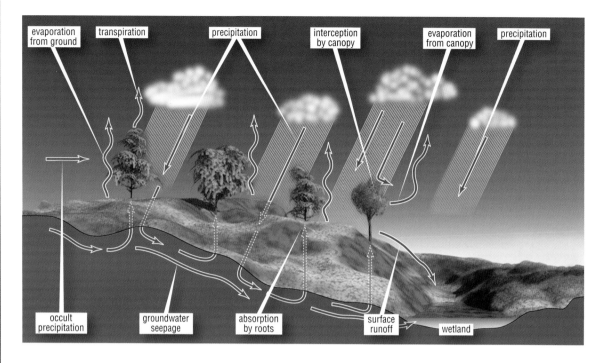

evaporation from ground
transpiration
precipitation
interception by canopy
evaporation from canopy
precipitation

occult precipitation
groundwater seepage
absorption by roots
surface runoff
wetland

The movement of water within a watershed

moves rapidly through the valley and on toward the sea. The slope of the valley floor and the presence of any obstacle blocking the movement of water out of the valley, together with the nature of the bedrock in the region, will influence the development of wetlands. These factors will be considered further in chapter 3.

In this example of water collection, it is assumed that all of the water landing in a catchment will move into the valley. This is very unlikely to be the case, however. The illustration shows the movement of water through a catchment and into a valley wetland. The precipitation arrives as rain or snow, but not all of it reaches the ground, especially if there is a forest cover over the slopes of the watershed. The canopy of the vegetation intercepts some rain or snow, and when the precipitation ceases some of this will evaporate back into the atmosphere without ever having reached the soil. Vegetation, then, acts almost like an umbrella, preventing some of the rainfall from reaching the regions beneath it. There are times, however, when vegetation can act in a different way and increase the amount of water arriving in a catchment: When mist and fog cover a forested mountain slope, water droplets condense upon the leaves and twigs of the trees and drip to the ground, adding to the water supply. Meteorologists call this *occult precipitation.* The water that arrives in this way is not recorded by standard equipment, such as the rain gauges that meteorologists set out to capture falling rain and snow. It is "hidden" from these instruments, hence the use of the term *occult.*

After water falls onto the ground or snow begins to melt, several things may happen to it. It may evaporate back into the atmosphere, or it may be soaked up by the soil and remain there, held by the spongelike action of small soil particles or the organic detritus, such as dead leaves and wood, within the soil. Some of the water in the soil is taken up by the roots of the growing plants. What remains may drain under the influence of gravity and eventually enter the streams or wetlands that form within the valley. How much of the water that arrives in a catchment moves on into the valley depends a great deal on the nature of the vegetation. Ecologists working in the Appalachian Mountains of the eastern United States have conducted a number of experiments in which the vegetation in a catchment has been changed in order to check on the consequences for water movement. Clearance of temperate deciduous forest (such as oak and hickory) from a catchment can increase the amount of water flowing into a valley by between 10 and 40 percent. This is because the canopy interception and the demands of plant transpiration have been removed. If oak forest is replaced by pine forest, however, the amount of water movement to the valley floor is reduced by 10 to 20 percent. This is because pine takes more water than does oak, partly because of its high transpiration, but also because as an evergreen it keeps its canopy all year round, so it can intercept and evaporate water even in winter when oak is bare.

The lesson for wetland ecologists from these experiments is that the vegetation in a watershed has a very large effect on water movements, so whether or not a wetland develops also depends upon the surrounding vegetation and land use.

Although wetlands are most abundant in low-lying regions that collect water from extensive watersheds, if precipitation is sufficient they can develop even on sloping grounds and elevated flat plateaus. Newfoundland, situated in the northeastern part of North America, has very high rainfall and generally cool temperatures through the year. This means that water does not evaporate quickly but constantly soaks the surface of the ground. Under these conditions wetlands can form even in unlikely situations, such as on gentle slopes where the constant water supply leads to saturation even though the surface water drains under the influence of gravity. Peat-forming wetlands can extend over hills as well as in valleys, forming a blanket over the landscape, which is why these wetlands are called *blanket bogs*. They are also found in northwestern Europe, some Southern Hemisphere islands, and even on high mountains close to the equator, where the combination of high rainfall and low temperatures prevails. These unusual wetlands, which will be covered in greater detail later in the chapter, illustrate how the pattern of wetland distribution in the landscape can sometimes be surprising.

Most wetlands in the landscape, then, are fed by the flow of water derived from a watershed or catchment, and these are called *rheotrophic* wetlands. The word *rheotrophic* is derived from Greek words and literally means fed by (-trophic) the flow (rheo-). Wetlands that derive their water supply solely from the rainfall, such as the blanket bogs of Newfoundland, are called *ombrotrophic* wetlands; *ombrotrophic* means fed by the rain (ombro-). When we consider the distribution of wetland types through the world, we find that warmer, drier regions contain only rheotrophic wetlands. Hotter and drier regions require a larger catchment to support a wetland because the limited water supply has to be gathered from a wider area.

Different kinds of wetlands

We have seen that it is possible to distinguish two main types of wetlands based upon their supply of water, rheotrophic and ombrotrophic. But each of these broad divisions contains a range of different wetlands. Each of these is described in turn in the following sections, beginning with the rheotrophic wetlands, proceeding to the ombrotrophic ones, and finally moving to the very distinctive wetlands associated with salty conditions around coasts and in certain inland situations.

Shallow freshwater wetlands

Freshwater lakes and ponds are found in all parts of the world, from the Arctic tundra to the equatorial regions. They can even occur in the arid parts of the world, as in the case of Lake Chad in the southern Sahara, but water bodies in the dry lands are often subject to changes in water level during drought. In such different climates freshwater lakes vary in the types of plants and animals they contain, but they have certain main features in common. Water more than 13 feet (4 m) in depth generally contains only microscopic forms of plant life, known as plankton, or free-floating aquatic plants that do not need to be rooted in the basal mud. Plants that take root at the bottom and have floating leaves, such as water lilies, can grow only in shallower water. This is because each leaf needs to have a stalk linking it to the buried stems in the mud, and 13 feet is the limit for this type of structure. Animals, however, are not limited in this way. From microscopic zooplankton to much

Reeds and cattails form a marsh around the edge of a pond.
(Courtesy of Jan Tyler)

The colonization of shallow water wetlands by plants. On the left the marsh plants are forming a floating mat of rhizomes and roots, while on the right the emergent plants are rooted in the sediment.

larger fish, mammals, or swimming birds, animals can occupy both shallow and deeper waters.

As the water becomes shallower at the edges of lakes, the penetration of sunlight to the bottom allows more plant species to grow on the submerged surface of the mud, though this depends in part how turbid, or murky, the waters are. If the water carries a heavy load of suspended material, such as silts, clays, or organic matter, then light penetration is poor and bottom-living plants can grow only in very shallow areas. Green algae in the form of fine filaments may occupy the boundary between the lake mud and the water above. Water that is seven feet (2 m) deep or less is often rich in floating-leaved aquatic plants and may also support *emergent* aquatic plants. These are tall plants that can root in the basal mud and produce stems that extend above the surface of the water. Reeds, cattails, and papyrus are examples of emergent aquatic plants.

Marshes and reed beds

A wetland that is dominated by emergent aquatic plants, such as reeds, sedges, and cattails, is called a marsh or a reed bed. Some parts of the Everglade wetlands in Florida are of this type and form extensive "rivers of grass." The water level is always above the mud surface, even in the dry season, and water flows through the dense mass of emergent stems, making its way toward the coast. The water, however, is shallow, usually less than seven feet (2 m) and in the drier periods sometimes less than one foot (30 cm). Beneath the surface of the water, the roots and new shoots of the vegetation form a dense mass, within which many types of invertebrate animals live. These are preyed upon by birds, fish, and amphibians that find shelter from their own predators within the complex of underwater tunnels and tall canopy above. For this reason the marsh habitats are important as breeding areas for fish, and tropical marshes are often vital for the survival of human fishing communities on lakeshores.

The emergent shoots of reeds may be as dense as 10 to 15 shoots per square foot (90 to 150 shoots per square meter). Their height can be as great as 10 to 13 feet (3 to 4 m) in the case of the common reed, or even higher in the case of tropical papyrus plants (up to 16 feet; 5 m). The overall structure or architecture of the habitat is much more complicated than that of a shallow pool. Not only is there an intricate pattern of tangled roots below the water level, but there is also a tall mass of vegetation, mainly in the form of vertical stems, above the water surface. In general, the more complicated the architecture of a habitat, the richer its biodiversity. Complicated architecture leads to new opportunities for animal life. Birds such as herons and bitterns can hunt fish and amphibians among the tall reeds while concealed from their enemies. Some birds, such as the European reed warbler (*Acrocephalus scirpaceus*), construct nests that hang like hammocks among the vertical stalks of reeds, suspended above the surface of the water.

Although marshes are usually created when emergent plants that are rooted in the basal mud invade shallow waters, they may also develop when floating mats of stems and roots invade (see the illustration on page 12). These often extend over relatively deep water, producing a flexible and unstable carpet that rises and falls with any change in the water depth. Floating rafts of this kind are particularly frequent in the tropical marshes dominated by papyrus. From the point of view of the animals living within them, the instability of the substrate is not a problem, as birds and amphibians are light enough to be supported by it, and the heavier mammals that occupy this habitat can usually swim well. The papyrus marshes of Lake Victoria and other lakes in East Africa are often affected by wave action resulting from storms on this very large lake. The effect of the waves splits up the papyrus rafts into floating islands that are set adrift on the waters of the lake. Similar floating "meadows" of aquatic vegetation can be found in the Amazon basin of Brazil, especially during periods of flood.

Marshes can form very extensive habitats. The saw-grass marshes of the Florida Everglades are impressively large areas of wetland; yet even these are dwarfed by the Esteros del Ibera in Argentina, a marsh-dominated wetland of almost 4,000 square miles (10,000 sq km), and the Sudd marshes of the Nile in southern Sudan of Africa, which cover around 40,000 square miles (100,000 sq km). In the temperate

Floating papyrus marsh, Lake Nabugabo, Uganda, East Africa. Papyrus marshes are found mainly in tropical wetlands. (Courtesy of Peter D. Moore)

regions of North America and Europe, patches of marshland tend to be much smaller and fragmented by agricultural drainage and development, but they still represent an important wildlife habitat.

Fens

Marshes have water on their surfaces even during the drought of summer, but fens have a water table below the surface of their soils. They are still wetland habitats and the soils are always moist to the touch, but in summer one must dig a pit to find the water level, which may be a foot (30 cm) below the surface. They are rheotrophic ecosystems, so the water is flowing into them from a catchment and through them to drainage streams. In winter and during floods they are covered by water, but they gradually dry out as the season proceeds.

The vegetation of a fen is usually more diverse than that of marshes, which are dominated by one or two robust and tall-growing species of reed or cattail. Instead, the vegetation of fens is shorter and often has a range of flowering plants that produce a more colorful aspect than the uniform marsh with its tall and dominant reeds. In the dry season air penetrates the soil, so plants that cannot cope with the permanent waterlogging of the marsh can grow in this habitat. The bird life of fens is more restricted than that of marshes, however, because the vegetation does not provide enough cover for bitterns or nesting locations for birds that need upright stalks to support their hammock nests. But amphibians are still abundant, and egrets and herons feed upon them in the fens. The shallow water of winter and the drier surface in summer allows more terrestrial grazing animals, such as deer, to use the fen as a source of food.

Fens come in a very wide range of different forms. They are dependent on their watersheds for a supply of water and also of chemical elements, so the supply of chemical nutrients to the vegetation varies with the geology of the catchment (see "Geology and water chemistry," pages 46–49). Some fens have an abundant supply of the nutrient elements needed for plant growth and they are called *rich fens*. Others, the *poor fens*, are supplied with weak chemical solutions because the

Aapa fen in northern Finland. Raised ridges that run along the contours cross these wetlands, and this is why they are sometimes called string bogs.
(Courtesy of Peter D. Moore)

surrounding rocks have poor concentrations of these elements. The diversity of plant and animal life varies with the richness of the mineral supply.

Fens are found throughout the world, wherever water gathers and flows from a catchment. Even in the apparently dry conditions of sand dunes, both inland and coastal, damp hollows can produce a fen. These special kinds of fens are called *dune slacks,* and they are often very rich in plant and animal diversity. The coastal dune slacks may experience seepage of seawater, resulting in a slightly saline, or brackish, habitat that supports a very specialized range of creatures. In cool temperate northern regions fens can be very extensive, and they show distinct surface patterns when viewed from the air. Flying over Canada or Scandinavia and Russia, one can make out valley fens with conspicuous stripes arranged across their surfaces. In Europe these are called *aapa fens,* while in North America they are often referred to as "string bogs." In fact, the string bogs are not true bogs at all, but are fens. The stripes are caused by raised ridges three feet (100 cm) above the water table that run across the slope of the fen, along its contours. These ridges may be sufficiently dry for trees such as black spruce to grow upon them. The ridges are separated by low-lying pools, often covered by bog mosses (genus *Sphagnum*). From the air the color contrast between the ridges and pools is very apparent because of the differences in vegetation and the strips of open water. It can be quite difficult to walk across such wetlands because occasionally the higher ridges come to an abrupt end, forcing anyone trying to cross the mire to retrace their steps to find a way through the maze. Water runs down the slope of the wetland, meandering along the pools and occasionally cutting through gaps in the ridges to move to the next level down. This flowing water defines the wetland as a rheotrophic fen.

Spring mires

A very distinctive type of fen habitat develops in mountain regions where slopes can be steep and where water occasionally seeps out of the ground because of outcrops of impermeable, waterproof rocks. Springs are often the sources of streams and rivers, but before the running water erodes into the soil and rock and forms its own streambed, it may move gently over the surface of the ground and create a small wetland, rich in plant and animal life. If the water has high concentrations of lime (calcium carbonate), then this compound can become encrusted to form extensive limy deposits, called *tufa*. Plants grow among the tufa deposits and create an intricate mix of organic peat and lime that can grow into large hummocks. How big these peaty masses grow depends upon the quantity and the force of the springwater that bubbles up from below, but heights of around 20 feet (6 m) are known.

Spring mires can be located among alpine vegetation on high mountains or within belts of coniferous or deciduous forest. Periodically, they may burst and erode, leading to unstable soils and constant disturbance, and this is one of the features that makes them of great interest to conservationists. In those parts of the world where glaciers once extended, around 20,000 years ago (including Canada, parts of the northern United States, northern Europe, and parts of northern Asia), forest has subsequently expanded as the climate has become warmer and the glaciers have retreated. As a result, many of the alpine plants and invertebrate animals have been lost in the more southerly parts of their range. But where spring mires have created instability, the forest has never been able to establish complete cover, and these small pockets of wet, eroding soils have created the right conditions for the local survival of the alpine survivors, or *relicts* of the Ice Age. Spring mires are not only rich in species but often contain very rare plants, mollusks, and insects that now have scattered, fragmented distribution patterns.

Swamps

Marshes and fens are covered by herbaceous, nonwoody vegetation. Swamps, on the other hand, are dominated by trees. Relatively few trees are able to cope with extremely wet soils, but some have proved very successful, such as the tamarack of the northern regions and the bald cypress of Florida. Marshes and fens can gradually become drier, in which case trees may invade them. Alders (*Alnus* species) and willows (*Salix* species) are particularly successful in establishing wet woodlands as wetlands develop, a habitat that is given the name *carr* in Europe. Swamp forest is also found in the low-lying floodplains of rivers, as is the case in the southeastern parts of North America. The Great Dismal Swamp of Virginia and North Carolina is 80 square miles (200 sq km) in extent and bears forest rich in Atlantic white cedar (*Chamaecyparis thyoides*) and tupelo (*Nyssa sylvatica* variety *biflora*), while the Big Cypress Swamp of southern Florida covers 1,500 square miles (4,000 sq km) and is dominated by bald cypress (*Taxodium distichum*), dwarf cypress, and slash pine (*Pinus elliottii*).

Swamps, together with marshes, form the most important and widely distributed of the tropical wetland types. In northern Australia, the Kakadu National Park is largely composed of swampland, containing coolibah trees (*Eucalyptus microtheca*) and river red gum (*Eucalyptus camaldulensis*). Southeast Asia is also rich in swamps, especially in the coastal regions. The Amazon basin in South America is subject to seasonal flooding as the snow of the Andes Mountains melts in the spring. Extensive swamps are then formed over patches of the floodplain as the river overflows its banks and engulfs the surrounding forest. In India the swamp of Bharatpur is world famous for its great variety of wildfowl, storks, and herons. In Africa the Okavango Swamp is seasonal, its waters spreading out over the edge of the Kalahari Desert in northern Botswana.

Water channels and river courses that run through the swamps are constantly changing their course as they undergo periodic floods and surges. Where water flows slowly on a

Swamps are dominated by trees, while marshes are dominated by herbaceous plants, such as reeds, sedges, and cattails. (Courtesy of Dan Brandenburg)

gentle incline, it tends to create channels that meander in wide bends. When a flood surge occurs, the water may take shortcuts, carving out new and straighter channels and leaving parts of the old winding channel isolated in crescent-shaped lakes, called oxbows. These still and open pools within the swamp add to the diversity of habitats and create new opportunities for aquatic plants and animals in the open-water gaps in the general forest cover.

The presence of trees in a wetland provides added spatial complexity to the habitat, and consequently more animals are able to inhabit it. The trees provide perching, roosting, feeding, and nesting sites for many bird species, including the storks, ibises, and herons that hunt in the marshes. The submerged parts of trees provide a complex underwater habitat where a greater range of fish can find shelter. The wealth of life in the canopy and in the water then provides food for large predators, including alligators, crocodiles, anacondas, and jaguars. So the swamps of the Tropics are among the most productive and diverse wetlands on Earth.

Tropical swamp in the rain forest of the Lower Kikori Basin, Papua New Guinea. One of the most important trees along water channels is the pandan (Pandanus species). *(Courtesy of Gerry Ellis/ Minden Pictures)*

Pothole mires and quaking bogs

Parts of North America and northern Russia that are far from the ocean are littered with small wetlands that occupy hollows, each of only a few acres in extent (usually less than 10 acres; four ha). These are areas that were once covered by the glacial ice sheets of the last ice age and were left bare as the ice retreated. But the ice did not move northward as a single, retreating mass; it left behind small pockets of melting ice in the form of ice blocks and islands in the landscape. Some of these fragmented ice masses were partially buried by the ground-down rocks and detritus carried in by the glaciers, so when the ice melted away it left a pit filled with water. These scattered pits were the origin of the pothole mires.

Over the 10,000 years since these pothole wetlands were formed, they have become filled in with soils eroding from their edges, so they are now shallow, usually less than three feet (1 m) in depth. They are surrounded by rings of marshes and fens that develop as the infilling proceeds, and the accompanying vegetation provides cover for breeding wildfowl, particularly ducks. The mires' importance for breeding ducks is so great that in the North American prairie region, the pothole wetlands are referred to as the "duck factory." The region that contains this wealth of wildfowl production includes southern Canada (Alberta, Saskatchewan, and Manitoba) and the northern part of the United States prairie region (Iowa, Minnesota, the Dakotas, and Montana).

One of the most distinctive features of the pothole mires is that each occupies a separate, small catchment, and these are not linked by channels. This is particularly apparent from the air, when the patches of open water form a speckled pattern over the landscape. The wetlands are filled by rainfall when conditions are wet, especially in the spring as snow melts, and then become drier as the heat of summer causes the water to evaporate. The underlying soils are nonporous; otherwise the water would simply sink into the ground. The prairie pothole wetlands are generally underlain by clays. Even so, the heat of summer can cause the water levels to fall, and in some cases surface water disappears entirely, leaving muddy hollows.

Some potholes can be deep and steep-sided, originating from large blocks of ice deeply buried in the ground. This

Prairie pothole wetland, Sam Ordway Nature Conservancy Park, South Dakota. These wetlands are famous for their breeding ducks, but the nest shown here belongs to a western grebe (Aechmophorus occidentalis). *(Courtesy of Jim Brandenburg/ Minden Pictures)*

type of hollow develops in a distinctive way, with the edge vegetation of reeds, sedges, or cattails forming a floating mat (see the illustration) that extends out over the deep water and eventually can cover the entire water surface. The colonizing vegetation may be gradually replaced; if the water is acidic, then bog mosses may take over, or the floating carpet may even support trees, such as white cedars. Often a small pool of open water remains at the very center of the mire, providing evidence that this is indeed the way in which the wetland has developed. The surface quakes when you walk across it because the vegetation carpet may only be a few feet thick and it overlies a body of water. This is why this type of wetland is sometimes called a *quaking bog*. If a person jumps up and down on it, the trees sway and bend as waves pass

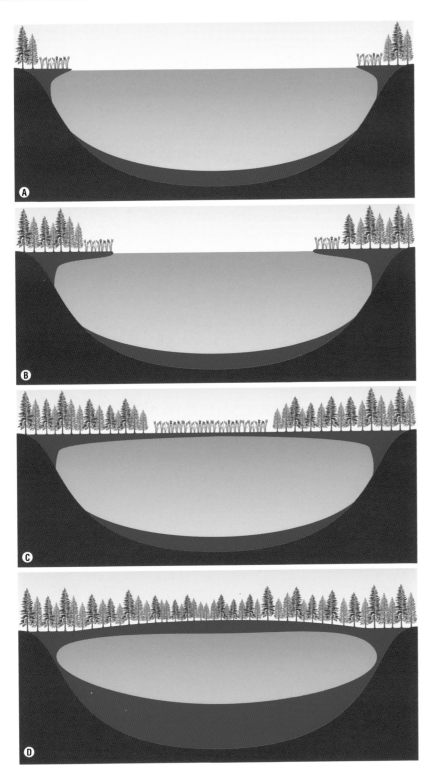

The development of a quaking bog. Small, steep-sided basins can be colonized by floating vegetation around their edges before the central part of the basin has become filled by sediments (stages A and B). The floating raft of vegetation will eventually cover the entire lake (C), forming a floating mat of rhizomes and peat (D). Invasion of bog mosses (genus Sphagnum) can then lead to the development of elevated, ombrotrophic bog on top of the raft. This may become invaded by trees.

along the floating surface. Quaking bogs are more common in the eastern part of North America, from eastern Canada to New England, and are also present in the western parts of Europe.

Raised bogs

The word *bog* is often used very casually, being applied to almost any wet ecosystem in which peat is being formed. But its use by wetland scientists is much more specific. A bog is an ombrotrophic peat land, which means that the sole input of water is from precipitation; no water draining through soil enters the ecosystem. This is the case if the surface of the vegetation is elevated above the level of water in the ground surrounding the bog. This occurs when peat has built up to such an extent that the surface of the bog is raised. One of the wetland types that falls into this category is the raised bog, or domed mire. This is an impressive peat land, which is most often found in large, flat valleys or floodplains, or in the estuaries of rivers. The dome of the mire can be a mile (1.6 km) or more across, and the general shape is like an inverted saucer, with the center of the peat land raised up to an elevation 30 feet (10 m) or more above the mire margin (see the illustration). Sometimes, as in the central plain of Ireland, raised bogs are found in groups along a river valley,

Cross section of a raised bog. The sequence of the different sediments reflects the course of successional development that this complex habitat has undergone over the course of several thousand years.

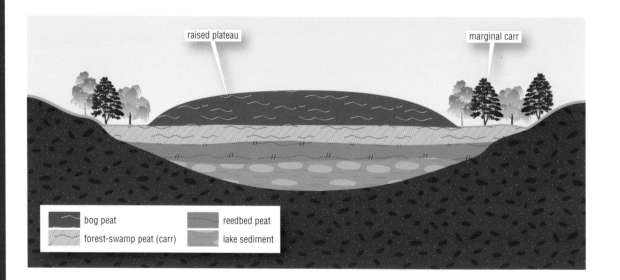

raised plateau

marginal carr

- bog peat
- forest-swamp peat (carr)
- reedbed peat
- lake sediment

with the whole landscape dominated by these extensive masses of peat land.

Raised bogs are found in many parts of North America, especially in the west and in the east of the cool temperate zone. They are similarly found throughout northern Europe and Russia, being most frequent in the maritime regions on the western and eastern parts of the continents. In the Southern Hemisphere they are found in the southern tip of South America and in New Zealand. In most maritime regions close to the sea, the raised bogs are usually treeless, which is when their great extent and their remarkable shape are most evident. In more continental regions, far from the influence of coastal winds and rain, trees grow over the dome of the bog, forming a bog forest growing on top of the masses of peat. In Alaska lodgepole pine (*Pinus contorta*) is a frequent inhabitant of raised bogs, whereas in eastern raised bogs black spruce (*Picea mariana*) and tamarack (*Larix laricina*) are more usual. In the case of the treeless raised bogs, the surface is dominated by bog mosses (genus *Sphagnum*), together with various sedges and dwarf shrubs, including many members of the heather family (Ericaceae), such as leatherleaf (*Chamaedaphne calyculata*) and bog rosemary (*Andromeda polifolia*). The surface is not uniform, however, but consists of open pools of water surrounded by flat green surfaces of floating mosses and by ridges and hummocks of sedges and evergreen dwarf shrubs.

Raised bogs, being entirely dependent on rain and snow for their water supply, can develop only where precipitation is high and evaporation low. This is why they are most abundant in cool northern regions, where low temperature keeps evaporation to a minimum. Their greater abundance in the more maritime parts of continents is due to the higher precipitation that usually occurs close to oceans. In the northern cool temperate zone a minimum of 19 inches (48 cm) of precipitation a year is needed if raised bogs are to develop. In Chile, at the southern tip of South America, only areas with at least 24 inches (48 cm) of rain a year have raised bogs, while in the warmer climate of New Zealand 50 inches (127 cm) of rain are needed for raised bog development. In a warm climate higher rainfall is required to support such a tall dome of peat.

Walking across the surface of a raised bog can be hazardous because only the hummocks can bear the weight of a human, and stepping on the green lawns of moss can lead to disaster. The pools are often many feet in depth and have bare peat bases that are soft. It is difficult to appreciate the pattern of these pools and hummocks from the ground surface, but from the air it becomes apparent. Pools in the center of the dome—where the surface is often quite flat, forming a plateau—are relatively circular in shape and scattered uniformly. But nearer the edge of the dome, where the peat begins to slope downward, the pools become more linear and follow the lines of the contours, forming a series of broken concentric rings around the dome. This is reminiscent of the linear patterns of pools and ridges on aapa fens (string bogs). Occasionally, an entire raised bog develops on a gently sloping surface, and this results in the highest point of the dome being off-center, situated toward the upper part of the slope. In this case the pools form a series of crescent-shaped structures as the peat slopes away from the high point, and the peat land is called an *eccentric bog*. Underlying geology influences the way in which pools are formed and develop (see "Geology and wetland landscapes," pages 42–46).

Although raised bogs are ombrotrophic mires, they are often situated in broad valleys through which water flows, so they are usually surrounded by rheotrophic mires, such as fens or marshes. These rheotrophic surroundings are called the *lagg* of the mire, and the sloping edges of the raised bog are termed the *rand.* Although the raised bog is not exceptionally rich in species of plant and animal, the species that occur there are highly specialized, being able to live under very low nutrient conditions. All elements entering the ecosystem arrive in the rainfall, so waters on the bog surface are acid and nutrient poor. Even some plants have to resort to digesting insects to enhance their nutrient supply. Because of their distinctive flora and fauna, the raised bog ecosystems are highly regarded by conservationists. Raised bogs have usually taken around 6,000 years or more to develop, which means that they are effectively irreplaceable.

Blanket bogs

In conditions of exceptionally high rainfall, accompanied by low temperature, and hence low evaporation, peat can form on mountain ridges and summits. Like the raised bogs, blanket bogs are ombrotrophic, but their hydrology (the way in which water moves through them) is more complicated because they stretch like a blanket over the landscape, so that they occupy hilltops, slopes, and valleys. In the valleys they receive drainage water from the slopes, so these parts of the peat land are rheotrophic and receive an enriched nutrient supply as a consequence. Like the raised bogs, however, their vegetation is composed of species that can cope with very low nutrient supplies. Trees are absent from blanket bogs, for these peat lands develop only in extremely oceanic, windy regions where trees find it difficult to grow.

Studies in western Europe, where some of the world's best examples of blanket bogs are found, suggest that the mountain regions now occupied by blanket bogs were once covered

Blanket bog at Silver Flowe, southeast Scotland. Blanket bogs occur only in regions of high rainfall, but given that, they can develop even over sloping ground. (Courtesy of Peter D. Moore)

with stunted trees and open forest. The soils beneath the blanket of peat are usually rich in charcoal, suggesting that the former woodland cover was removed and burned. It is likely that grazing animals then kept the landscape clear of trees as the peat began to accumulate in soils that were increasingly wet because of the forest removal (see "Wetland distribution in the landscape," pages 7–10). Once a peat cover had been formed, tree seeds would no longer be able to germinate and establish themselves, so the blanket bog became secure. It is not known whether blanket bogs in all parts of the world have been assisted in their development by human activities. It is possible that the additional assistance given by prehistoric human cultures was needed only where the climate was marginal for blanket bog formation. Once the peat has begun to form, it can develop to a depth of 20 feet (6 m) or more in the hollows and as much as 10 feet (3 m) on plateaus and slopes. The process by which blanket bogs evolve is shown diagrammatically in the illustration.

Blanket bogs are found not only in western Europe but also in eastern Canada, particularly Newfoundland; in Iceland; around the Pacific Rim, from Alaska to Kamchatka; and also in the Southern Hemisphere in Tierra del Fuego, New Zealand, and some southern islands, such as the Falklands. The most surprising site for blanket bog development is the Ruwenzori range of mountains in western Uganda, almost on the equator. All of these regions have very heavy rainfall, which is clearly required if peat is to form on sloping, well-drained ground. High rainfall is often associated with mountain ranges and with proximity to the ocean, which is why

(opposite page) *A series of profile diagrams showing the development of a blanket mire landscape. A. Hilly, wooded country in an oceanic climate with high precipitation has mires developing only in hollows. B. Over the course of centuries these low-lying mires undergo succession and become colonized by vegetation leading to wooded swamps. C. Prehistoric human forest clearance, together with increasing climatic wetness, leads to the development of blanket mires, initiating on hilltops and plateaus. D. Further forest clearance, fire, and grazing by domestic animals leads to a complete blanket of peat land covering hilltops, slopes, and valleys.*

water
bog peat
wood peat
reed-swamp peat
lake clays
bedrock

blanket bogs are most common in such regions. In Britain, for example, blanket bogs develop only where the rainfall is greater than 50 inches (125 cm) per year. In the south of Britain this amount of rainfall is limited to the western hill regions above 1,400 feet (430 m), but on the coasts of western Ireland and western Scotland blanket bogs can develop even at sea level. Perhaps the overall humidity and low evaporation rate are more important than the actual rainfall. Regions where blanket bogs are present usually experience at least 225 days in the year when some rain falls.

Arctic wetlands

We have seen that the polar regions receive descending air masses in the general atmospheric circulation (see "Where on Earth are the wetlands?" pages 3–7). Cold, descending air releases little precipitation, so the regions close to the North and South Poles are virtually deserts. Despite this fact, the Arctic regions are rich in wetlands. Under cold conditions, evaporation of water is very slow, hence soils are saturated and water accumulates in pools and channels. In the long Arctic winter, however, all water is frozen, and temperatures in the soil remain so low even in summer that the subsoil never thaws. Below a depth of about 12 to 15 inches (30 to 40 cm) in the High Arctic lies the *permafrost,* a layer of constant ice that forms an impermeable barrier to downward water movement.

When the upper layers of snow and soil thaw in the spring, therefore, the water they contain either remains in place in pools or drains over the surface in channels. When winter comes again and the water in the channels freezes, the ice that is formed expands and forces itself downward like a wedge into the soil. Ice wedges of this sort develop in intricate patterns over the surface of the landscape, producing polygons of raised ground surrounded by drainage channels. Even the raised areas are wet enough to allow peat to develop, but usually only to a depth of about 20 inches (50 cm). These are the *polygon mires* of the tundra. The centers of many of the polygons are slightly depressed, so they carry a wetland vegetation of their own, usually sedges and cotton grasses, while the edges of the polygons that form the banks of the ditches are raised and therefore drier. In other polygons the center is elevated into a shallow dome, and the peat over the central parts may erode, leaving bare surfaces (see the illustrations).

Many migratory birds, especially wildfowl and waders, arrive in summer to breed in this complex pattern of wetlands. The drier ridges and banks provide the birds with safe conditions in which to nest and lay their eggs, while the wetter areas provide a wealth of food. Many of North America's wild geese, such as brant geese (*Branta bernicla*), white-fronted geese (*Anser albifrons*), and snow geese (*Chen caerulescens*), breed in these Arctic wetlands, as do the wild trumpeter swans (*Cygnus buccinator*). They all depart south before winter when the entire region becomes frozen over.

To the south of these polygon wetlands, where the tundra meets the first stunted trees of birch and pine, another type of Arctic wetland is found called *palsa mire*. The word *palsa*

Profile of Arctic polygonal mires. A. A low-center polygon mire in which the central region of the polygon is depressed and holds water. B. A high-center polygon mire in which the mid-region of the polygon is elevated by the frozen soil (permafrost) and is covered by draining and eroding peat.

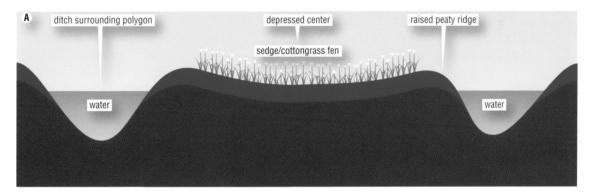

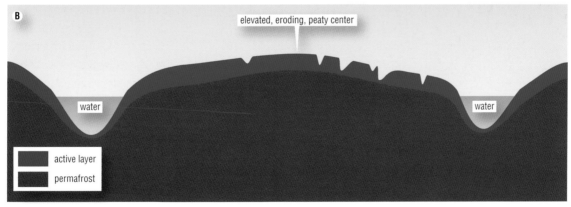

comes from the Finnish language, and these mires are frequently found in northern Finland, as well as in Arctic Canada and Russia. In general appearance palsa mires look like a patchwork of large mounds among flat areas of sedge, together with open pools. The mounds are often six to 10 feet (2 to 3 m) in height and may be up to 150 feet (45 m) in diameter. If a person were to dig down in one of these mounds, they would pass through just a foot or two of peat and then come to a mass of ice. This ice core extends right down into the subsoil below the palsa mound. The patchwork of the palsa mire is caused by a constant cycle of palsa development; some mounds are actively growing, while others are decaying. Wetland scientists have expended much effort in trying to understand the process of their formation. The diagram illustrates the cycle of palsa development and decay.

Palsa mounds originate in flat sedge meadows. In winter the entire area becomes frozen, but a layer of snow partially insulates the ground. If any location is slightly elevated because of local peat formation or the development of a series of tussocks of vegetation, then the tundra winds blow the snow away and such spots freeze to a great depth. When spring comes, these locations are the last to thaw out and may not melt at all. Ice expands as it forms, so these cold patches begin to push upward as they develop, which means that less snow collects in winter and they become even colder. So the process continues, and the growing ice core eventually forms a palsa mound. As the surface of the mound becomes raised above its surroundings, it becomes drier and

(opposite page) *The rise and fall of a palsa mound. 1. The Arctic wetland surface is fairly flat. 2. Any slight irregularity results in poor snow cover and less insulation on the raised area, so ground ice persists through the summer and swells. 3. The ice core continues to grow and raises the mire surface above the surroundings, as a result of which it becomes drier and clothed with dwarf shrubs and light-reflecting, white lichens. 4. Eventually the top of the palsa begins to erode as a consequence of water runoff, and bare, black peat is exposed. This dark surface absorbs sunlight in summer and instigates an ice-core meltdown. 5. The palsa collapses, leaving a pool surrounded by a circular rampart.*

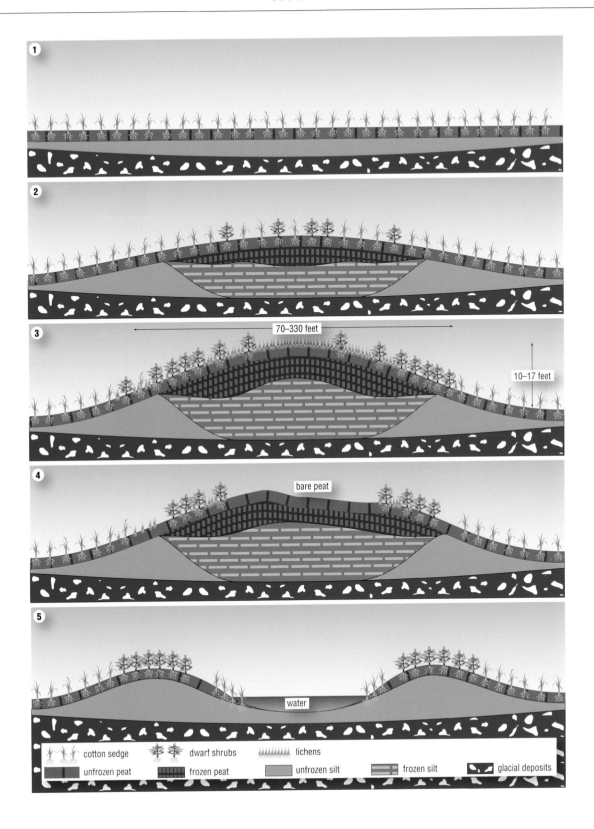

1

2

3
70–330 feet
10–17 feet

4
bare peat

5
water

cotton sedge	dwarf shrubs	lichens		
unfrozen peat	frozen peat	unfrozen silt	frozen silt	glacial deposits

the vegetation changes. At first lichens colonize the rising mound and, being light in color, they reflect much of the summer sunlight, keeping the palsa cool in summer. But eventually they are replaced by the darker vegetation of dwarf shrubs, and these absorb sunlight, causing the upper parts of the ice core to melt in summer. The vegetation and the thin peat layer over the mound then begin to break up and the dark peat is exposed, leading to more heat uptake and faster meltdown. The palsa mound then collapses quite rapidly as the entire ice core melts and a pool is formed. The pool becomes colonized by sedges, and the whole cycle begins again.

The generally cold climate is obviously an important factor in palsa formation—otherwise the ice cores could not survive the summer. Palsas are found only where the average yearly temperature is less than 32°F (0°C) and where the summer growing season is less than 120 days. Changing climate in the past has evidently affected the initiation of palsa development because palsa mounds are often found in groups of similar age. Conservationists are now concerned that the current change in climate experienced by the Arctic will lead to a loss of this distinctive type of wetland.

Coastal wetlands

Coastal regions can be roughly divided into two types, one in which material is being constantly removed, or eroded, and the other in which material is being constantly deposited. Erosional shores can be spectacular because they often develop steep, rocky cliffs where the waves beat against the land and remove all loose material. Depositional shores are usually flatter and quieter, often developed in sheltered locations in bays and estuaries, where wave action is less frequent and water moves more slowly. It is in waters of this type that coastal wetlands are most likely to develop.

In the temperate zone the most common type of coastal wetland is the *salt marsh*. These are most frequently found in the sheltered area behind shingle ridges or barrier islands, or in the brackish conditions of estuaries, where rivers enter the ocean. On their seaward side they usually have extensive flat areas of mud, often derived from organic materials carried down by the river from terrestrial ecosystems farther upstream. As the flow of the river meets the incoming tide, the waters flow more slowly. The slow-moving water can no longer support its heavy load of eroded silts, clays, and organic materials, so it deposits these sediments as mud. The accumulating mud is colonized by vegetation, such as sea grass (*Zostera* species), which grows low down on the shore and may spend all its life immersed, or by succulent glasswort (*Salicornia* species) or cordgrasses (*Spartina* species) that grow on the higher muds and are left exposed at low tide. The presence of plants slows the water even more, so even the fine particles fall out of suspension and build up the mud more rapidly. In this way the mud surface is raised and an increasing number of plants are able to occupy the area, eventually leading to extensive meadows of flowering plants, including salt marsh grasses, sea lavender, plantains, and asters. These flat plains are flooded less frequently by the tide as mud continues to accumulate and their surfaces continue to rise. But less frequent flooding by the sea means that the input of mud is reduced, so a fairly stable type of marsh eventually develops that experiences flooding less than 100 times a year. The vegetation of the salt marsh forms a series of zones that are determined by how many times in the year they receive floodwater from the ocean, and each zone has its particular community of tolerant plants.

The surge of the tide entering a salt marsh contains a lot of energy, and this moving water carves out creeks that cut deep into the marsh. In the very high spring tides the seawater overflows the banks of the creeks and carries sediments onto the high marsh, but in time these floods become less frequent. Water drains from the marsh as the tide recedes, but some may remain in isolated pools, called *pans,* which develop into small ecosystems of their own. Conditions in these pans are extreme. Following tidal flooding, they contain salt water, and if the flood tide is followed by hot, dry conditions, they evaporate to create extremely saline pools. But it is also possible that they will experience heavy rain, in which case the salinity of the pans falls rapidly and the water can become almost completely fresh. Water temperature also changes quickly at such times, so only animals that

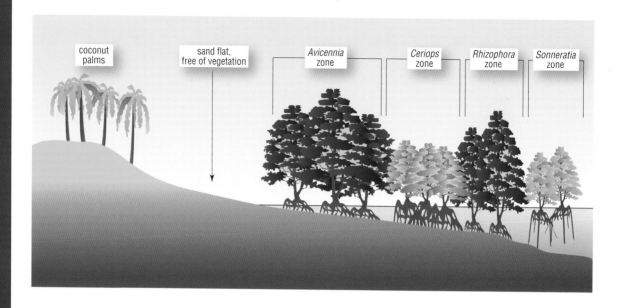

coconut palms

sand flat, free of vegetation

Avicennia zone

Ceriops zone

Rhizophora zone

Sonneratia zone

Profile of mangrove zonation in East Africa. Different species of tree are best suited to different depths of water and different salinities. Hence a zonation pattern arises, the precise pattern of which varies in different parts of the world. The total distance between the open ocean and the upper limit of the mangrove swamp is approximately one mile.

are capable of very wide tolerance to salinity and temperature are able to survive in the pans.

In tropical climates coastal wetlands are dominated by woody trees rather than by herbs, such as grasses. Very few of the world's trees are capable of growing in saline waters, and the coastal wetlands of the Tropics are dominated by just one group of trees, which form the *mangrove swamps.* Like salt marshes, mangrove swamps have a pattern of zonation (see the illustration). Different species of trees have different tolerances to salinity and water depth, so the pioneer species that invade the deeper waters give way to less tolerant species that live closer to the land. Unlike the salt marshes, however, the tree dominants provide a much more complicated architecture, both above and below the water, than do the turf-forming herbs of salt marshes. The tree canopy contains many opportunities for animals, ranging from bees to monkeys, to thrive. The water that flows among the branching roots of the mangrove trees provides a breeding ground for many fishes and a feeding ground for reptiles. When the tide recedes, the exposed mud among the mangrove roots represents another habitat where crabs and mudskippers can exploit the food resources. (Chapter 4 examines the adaptations of these creatures.)

The coastal plains of some parts of Southeast Asia, especially on the islands of Borneo, New Guinea, and Sumatra, have a coastal wetland that is unique. In the estuarine plains of the great rivers, a wetland develops that is dominated by forest and yet accumulates peat. Under conditions of very heavy rainfall throughout the year in these equatorial regions, the falling leaves and branches of trees fail to decompose, and they accumulate as a growing mass of organic detritus. Over the course of time there develops a kind of massive compost heap, often several miles across and up to 50 feet (15 m) deep, all covered by dense forest with trees growing to heights of 150 feet (45 m). Once they are raised so far above the surface of the ground, these peat lands are no longer fed by groundwater but are reliant on the rainfall for their water supply. They must therefore be regarded as ombrotrophic wetlands. These are among the least known of all of the world's wetlands yet are among the most threatened by exploitation, both for timber and peat. They contain a wealth of wildlife, including a rare great ape, the orangutan. They are also of considerable geological interest because these tropical, ombrotrophic peat lands are the closest existing wetland to the ancient coal-forming swamps of Carboniferous times (see "Geology of ancient wetlands," pages 64–66).

Coastal wetlands, both temperate and tropical, are vulnerable because of their proximity to the sea. Storms and tsunamis (see the "Storms and tsunamis" sidebar on page 38) can result in flooding and erosion of these fragile ecosystems.

Changing wetlands

One thing that all of these different types of wetland have in common is that they are constantly changing. All wetlands are developing as time passes. Lakes and ponds are filling in as silt washes in from eroding watersheds and organic matter is produced by the resident plants. When emergent plants establish themselves in a shallow lake, they slow the movement of water, and this leads to more sediment becoming deposited. A bed of reeds in a marsh ecosystem is a very effective trap for sediments. In one study of a marsh, scientists

Storms and tsunamis

Wetlands that develop in coastal regions are prone to certain risks that are not experienced by inland wetlands. Storms, especially when coupled with very high tides, can result in flooding and damage to low-lying coastal areas. In the temperate regions deep depressions are accompanied by strong winds that circulate around a center of low pressure, spinning clockwise in the Northern Hemisphere and counterclockwise in the Southern Hemisphere. These winds create strong wave action, especially when they cross extensive areas of ocean before striking the shore. The salt marshes of the east coast of the United States are especially prone to such storms, as are those of western of Europe. In the North Sea region, the problem is exacerbated by its funnel shape, southward-moving waters being forced into the constricted sea between Denmark, Germany, and the Netherlands in the east, and the British Isles in the west. When storms accompany high tides in this region, they frequently flood the low-lying coasts, including coastal wetlands and even those farther inland, as in the fenland region of eastern England.

Tropical storms, or typhoons, are even more ferocious, generating higher wind speeds, as in the devastating Hurricane Katrina of August 2005. Regions such as the Caribbean and the Gulf of Mexico, or the Bay of Bengal in the north of the Indian Ocean are particularly prone to such storms and the flooding of coastal wetlands. Mangrove swamps are particularly susceptible to such storms, but they are also very resilient, soon recovering from damage.

Tidal waves, or tsunamis, are even more devastating. These are usually generated by undersea earthquakes or volcanic eruptions that produce shock waves transmitted at very high velocities through the oceans. Surface waves are produced, but these are not normally very large when traveling through deep water. They become more massive and dangerous as they enter the shallower conditions around coastal regions, when the front of the wave is slowed and the rear of the wave catches up with it, creating a crest that can rise to 60 feet (20 m) or more. The Indian Ocean tsunami of December 26, 2004, was created by the shifting of the floor of the ocean to the west of Sumatra in Southeast Asia. The waves generated struck the neighboring coast of Sumatra with great force, flooding the low-lying lands and their settlements and destroying whole towns. The tsunami passed westward over the Indian Ocean, striking the island of Sri Lanka and the east coast of India, as well as the coast of Somalia on the east of Africa. The damage to wetlands caused by this natural disaster extended not only to the fringing mangrove swamps, but also to the coastal peat-forming mires.

found that a density of 10 to 15 shoots of reed per square foot (90 to 150 shoots per sq m) could trap four and a half pounds (2 kg) of sediment in a year. Obviously the rate of sediment accumulation varies not only with the density of the reeds but also with the quantity of suspended material in the waters passing through the marsh, but these figures demonstrate just how fast the sediment can build up beneath this wetland type.

The general principle this illustrates is that the presence of a plant in an ecosystem changes the physical conditions, and this change can lead to an alteration in the way that ecosystem develops. The presence of a reed, for example, leads to faster sedimentation, and as the mud surface comes nearer to the surface of the overlying water, other plants are able to colonize, and the whole nature of the community changes. Ecologists call this process of development *succession*. It takes place in very many different types of ecosystem, from sand dunes to fresh volcanic lava. The presence of one species actually assisting in the establishment of a different species is also a widespread occurrence, which is called *facilitation*. It is not, however, due to some kind of design within nature whereby one plant very generously helps another along, but is rather an inevitable outcome of a plant's presence changing the conditions. As things change, other species take advantage of the new set of conditions and may even outcompete and eliminate the species that has unwittingly assisted their establishment. A drying marsh, for example, where the sediment surface in summer comes close to the surface of the water above it, may become colonized by wetland trees, such as willows and alders. As the trees form a dense canopy, they shade the reeds that preceded them, and eventually the reeds die from lack of sunlight. Facilitation is followed by *competition*.

Facilitation and competition are the driving forces of succession, but they often take the ecosystem into unexpected lines of development. Consider the development of raised bogs (see pages 24–26). The early stages of succession are often similar to those just described; a lake becomes filled with sediment, assisted by the extension of marshes around its edges, and the marsh becomes shallower and forms fens or wooded swamps. In the cool temperate regions and under conditions of high rainfall, the succession can then take its unexpected turn as an unlikely plant takes over the succession, namely the bog moss sphagnum. This is a moss with remarkable properties of competition that is able to colonize swamp forests and to form lawns that dominate the forest floor. By changing the chemistry of the water and developing into spongelike masses on the ground, the bog moss creates conditions in which the tree seedlings are no longer able to establish themselves (see "Plants of the wetlands," pages 98–105). At this point the forest is doomed. Although trees may persist for a few more decades, their ultimate fate is sealed. Within a few centuries the tree cover will be reduced to a few stunted individuals, and the bog moss will have taken over dominance.

In fact, this is an oversimplification of the course of events because there are many species of bog moss. Each species has its own requirements in terms of water chemistry, surface wetness, the acidity, and the degree of shade. The different bog mosses often replace one another as the succession proceeds: With shade-tolerant species occurring at first, and shade-intolerant species replacing them as the trees die, the canopy opens, and full sunlight strikes the ground. Bog mosses do not require contact with the soil, so they can grow directly on top of the underlying layer of moss. Thus as they grow, the bog mosses form a spongy mass of peat beneath them that accumulates over the course of thousands of years, never fully decomposing but building up into the great dome of peat that forms the most characteristic feature of the raised bog ecosystem. The peats and sediments of the succession remain preserved beneath this dome and provide a direct source of evidence that allows the ecologist to trace the direction the process has taken (see the illustration on page 24).

Succession is common to all wetlands. No wetland is entirely stable, therefore, but is constantly changing. New conditions develop due not only to the activities of plants and animals, but also to the hazards of the natural environment. Floods and storms, lightning strikes and fire, hurricanes and windstorms, changing courses of streams and rivers, and seasonal changes in physical condition all create instability in wetlands. Alligators create muddy hollows of open water, beavers create dams and flood previously dry habitats, and roosting herons bring rich supplies of nutrients to areas that were once nutrient poor. All of these combine to produce a constant series of changes that typify wetlands. Perhaps it is their inherent instability that makes wetlands so rich in species and so fascinating to ecologists.

Conclusions

Wetlands occur in two main regions of the world, the combined cool temperate and Arctic zone, and the tropical zone. This can be accounted for by the movement of air masses in the atmosphere and the unequal distribution of rainfall over the Earth.

Wetlands need an abundant supply of water, and this may be derived directly from rainfall, as in the case of ombrotrophic wetlands, or, more often, from the collection of groundwater over an extensive catchment or watershed, as in the case of rheotrophic wetlands. Only under very high rainfall conditions can the ombrotrophic wetlands develop, but they are found in both tropical and temperate wetland zones. Under drier conditions rheotrophic wetlands predominate and form the only type of terrestrial wetland in the dry regions of the world.

Wetlands can be classified into a range of different types, including shallow freshwater, marshes, fens, swamps, pothole and quaking mires, bogs, Arctic mires, salt marshes, and mangroves. All of these have very different vegetation, animal life, and processes of development. But they all have in common a constant process of change as the course of succession proceeds. Succession itself is renewed by the occasional catastrophe that strikes wetlands in the form of storms, floods, fire, and wind, in addition to those changes created by the animals that inhabit them. The distribution and development of wetlands is complex, but by understanding these aspects of their ecology we are in a better position to conserve and manage this rich and precious resource.

CHAPTER 2

GEOLOGY OF WETLANDS

Geology is the study of rocks. The average person thinks of rocks as hard materials such as granite, limestone, and sandstone, but geologists also include softer materials in their definition of rocks. Silt, clay, mud, and peat are all relatively soft substances that accumulate on parts of the Earth's surface, and they are regarded as rocks by scientists who study geology. Geology is an important aspect of wetland studies for a variety of reasons. Wetlands lie on the surface of the Earth and are underlain by rocks; the extent of the wetlands, the chemistry of their waters, and the kind of sediments that build up within a wetland are therefore influenced by the underlying geology of the region.

Geology and wetland landscapes

Wetlands can develop only in regions where water accumulates, and this means that the ground underlying the wetland must be impervious to water. Some rocks are much more easily penetrated by water than others. Limestone, for example, absorbs water, so water gradually sinks through it. Water also dissolves limestone, especially if the water is acidic, which is usually the case for rainwater, and acidic drainage water excavates cracks, caves, and caverns that quickly carry away any water that lies on the surface of the rocks. Sandstone is made up of numerous sand grains compacted and cemented together, but there are usually tiny spaces remaining between the grains. Therefore water can seep through the rock and drain away. Granite is formed by volcanic activity, which produces a molten rock that subsequently cools and crystallizes. As a result all air spaces in the rock have been sealed, and it is impervious to water. Shale and slate are sedimentary rocks, meaning that, like sandstone, they have been formed either under the oceans or in former wetlands, where water-borne particles have been deposited and gradually compacted into rock. Unlike sandstone, which has undergone no further process following compaction, shale and slate have been heated to high temperatures because of nearby volcanic activity. The intense heat changes their form by sealing any pores in their structure, making them impervious to water. Thus the physical constitution of rocks plays an important part in determining whether a wetland can develop at a particular site. Where there is standing water in a valley, it is certain that the underlying ground is waterproof, resisting the tendency of water to soak downward under the influence of gravity and disappear beneath the surface.

Even porous rocks, however, can be made impervious if fine particles of material block up the pores. This can happen if the waters draining into a valley carry a load of eroded material from the catchment rocks, which settles onto the surface of the porous rocks and forms a layer that seals them. Clay consists of very fine particles, less than 0.00008 inches (2 μm), so they are easily carried long distances by moving waters. Many rocks contain embedded clay particles, including granite, so the erosion of these rocks in a catchment liberates clay into the drainage water. When the water arrives in the valley, some of these clay particles settle as the speed of the water decreases, and they may block up the pores in the underlying rocks and create a waterproof barrier that allows a wetland to develop. One other fine particle that can play a similar part in the formation of wetlands is charcoal. Charcoal consists of partially burned fragments of plant material that are very resistant to decay. Following a wildfire, charcoal particles are blown over the surface of soils and are often washed into valleys, where they accumulate as a black, waterproof layer, and this, like a clay layer, can lead to the development of wetland.

Underlying geology, therefore, including the softer materials such as silt, clay, and charcoal that can be deposited over the parent rocks below, provides the base on which wetlands can form. But the form of the landscape also has an effect on wetland development. Under conditions of very high rainfall, as seen in chapter 1, peat-forming wetlands may develop even on mountain ridges and slopes. However, wetlands are generally more abundant in hollows in the landscape, where water can accumulate. If we consider a region where the underlying bedrock is impervious to water (granite, shale, or slate, for example), then wetlands are most likely to be found in valleys or in hollows in the general landscape, as shown in the top illustration. Wetlands of this kind are called *topogenous,* which means that they are dependent on the topography (the shape and form) of the landscape. These are among the most abundant of wetland types, especially in regions where precipitation is not excessive and water can accumulate only when gathered together from a wider catchment.

A second type of wetland is the *soligenous* wetland, as shown in the middle illustration. This is similar to the topogenous wetland in that it lies in hollows, but it is fed by the emergence of water from the ground as a result of porous, water-laden rocks meeting impervious rocks below. Where the two come into contact, the water descending under the influence of gravity through the porous rocks is unable to continue its descent but is forced to move sideways over the surface of the impervious rock until it emerges as a line of springs. These springs then feed the wetland that develops along the line of the rock boundary and in the hollows that lie below that line. This type of wetland occurs only where two very different types of rock come together, as when limestone overlies shale, for example. When this occurs, the wetland that develops may have different water chemistry than appearances would suggest. In the case of limestone overlying shale, for example, water rich in calcium carbonate (lime) drains onto the surface of an acidic rock and creates an unexpectedly lime-rich wetland with distinctive flora and fauna.

A third type of wetland that is dependent on the general form of the landscape is the *floodplain* wetland, shown in the bottom of the illustration. This occurs in the lower parts of river valleys, where the landscape is broad and flat on either side of a river that often meanders down a gentle slope on its way to the ocean. At this stage in its development a river has often traveled great distances and has been joined by many tributaries, so its water is supplied by a wide catchment. If there are heavy rains over that catch-

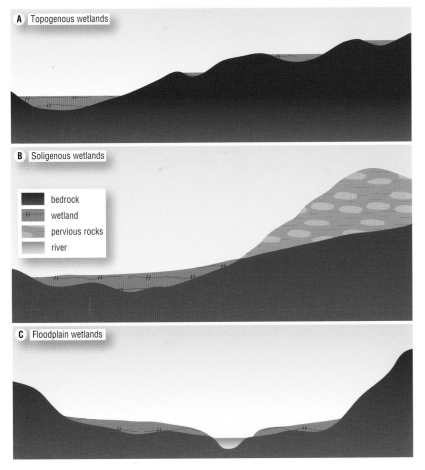

A Topogenous wetlands

B Soligenous wetlands

bedrock
wetland
pervious rocks
river

C Floodplain wetlands

Different types of wetland landscape and drainage patterns. A. Topogenous wetlands, where water accumulates in the low-lying regions on impervious rocks. B. Soligenous wetlands, where water soaks into a permeable rock, then emerges in spring lines and wetland when it comes into contact with an underlying impermeable rock. C. Floodplain wetlands develop in low-lying broad valleys, where floodwaters overflow the riverbanks and spread over the surrounding plain.

ment, or even over a small part of it, floodwater accumulates in the river channel and moves swiftly downriver. A sudden rush of water may lead to the river overflowing its banks and spreading out across the wide plain, the floodplain, on either side. Human populations have often settled these floodplains because their rich soils, frequently fertilized by the suspended sediments of the floodwaters, are ideal for agricultural development. The Nile in Egypt and the Mississippi in North America both have extensive floodplains that have been developed in this way. The floods that once spread over the flat landscape and supported wetlands have now been drained and the river channel embanked to prevent floods, and reservoirs have been constructed to control the movement of waters. These measures starve the floodplain wetlands of their water supply, so this type of wetland is becoming increasingly scarce.

Geology and water chemistry

The water that flows through a wetland is the source of nutrient elements for the plants and therefore is ultimately the basis of mineral nutrition for all the inhabitants of wetlands. The most abundant elements in living plants and animals are carbon and oxygen. Both of these elements are present in the atmosphere as the gases carbon dioxide

Acidity and pH

One of the most influential elements in water is hydrogen. Positively charged atoms of hydrogen, called hydrogen ions or protons, are the source of acidity in water. They are represented by the chemical symbol H^+. An acid can be defined as a compound that acts as a source of hydrogen ions. Hydrochloric acid has the formula HCl, and when this is dissolved in water it breaks up, or dissociates, into its component parts, each of which has a different electrical charge, H^+ and Cl^-. The same is true of all acids, such as sulfuric acid, nitric acid, carbonic acid, and even the organic acids such as malic acid. When dissolved in water (H_2O), all of them release hydrogen ions into their surroundings. Rainwater is acidic in reaction because it contains an excess of hydrogen ions. This is a consequence of carbon dioxide (CO_2) dissolving in airborne raindrops, creating carbonic acid (H_2CO_3):

$$H_2O + CO_2 \rightarrow H_2CO_3$$

Carbonic acid in water splits (dissociates) into two charged units, a hydrogen carbonate ion (negatively charged) and a hydrogen ion (positively charged):

$$H_2CO_3 \rightarrow HCO_3^- + H^+$$

The higher the concentration of hydrogen ions in water, the greater is its acidity. Chemists have devised a simple scale of acidity, the pH scale, which is easier to use than stating hydrogen ion concentration. The pH number is related to hydrogen ion concentration, but there are two complications to be borne in mind. First, it is negative. So the smaller the pH number, the higher the hydrogen ion concentration and the greater the degree of acidity. Second, it is logarithmic, so that one unit difference in pH value means

(CO₂) and oxygen (O₂), and are also easily dissolved in water, so there is not usually any problem in obtaining them. When the gases are in a dissolved state, however, they move (diffuse) much more slowly than in air, which means that they can be in short supply if the water itself is stagnant, causing problems (see "How do wetlands work?" pages 71–73). Hydrogen is also an important element in plants and animals, and its concentration in water has an important effect on many other chemical reactions, for hydrogen concentration controls the acidity, or pH, of the water (see sidebar).

10 times the concentration of hydrogen ions. A neutral solution, which is neither acid nor alkaline, has a pH of 7. A pH of less than 7 indicates acidity and one of more than 7 indicates alkalinity.

The illustration shows this scale of acidity. Lemon juice is acid and has a pH of 2. Ammonia is alkaline and has a pH of more than 12. Rich (calcareous) fens may have a pH close to 8; poor fens are closer to 4.5, and bogs may have a pH of 3.5 or below. Unpolluted rainwater with dissolved carbon dioxide has a pH of 5.4.

The pH scale, therefore, provides a simple index of acidity. It is easily measured using a colored dye, litmus, which turns red when the pH is low (acid) and blue when the pH is high (alkaline). Many other elements vary in their solubility and their behavior depending on pH, so this is a very important aspect of the chemistry of natural waters.

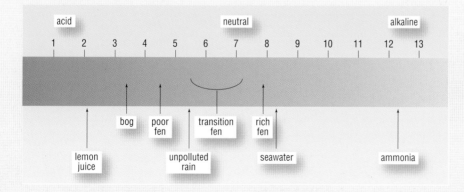

The pH scale

Nitrogen, as a major constituent of protein, is the next most important element. Protein comes in many different forms, some of it structural (as in the case of fingernails and hair) and some of it in the form of enzymes (large molecules within each cell that control all the reactions that take place there). Both plants and animals contain proteins, but they are generally more abundant in animal tissues, so animals need more nitrogen for building proteins than plants do. Because plant tissues are poorer in proteins than animals, herbivores (or vegetarians) either have to eat more material in order to obtain enough protein (and its contained nitrogen) or they have to be selective in the plant material they consume. (Beans, for example, contain more protein than lettuce.) In a wetland nitrogen may occur as a dissolved gas, but this is not available to plants and animals because nitrogen gas (N_2) is not at all reactive, and plants and animals are unable to convert it into protein. Some microbes, however, including the blue-green bacteria (cyanobacteria), are able to convert nitrogen gas into ammonia (NH_3) and then use this compound in the construction of protein. They are said to "fix" nitrogen. Cyanobacteria are quite common in wetlands, so their activity is important in increasing the fertility of waters.

Nitrogen is also present in the form of the nitrate ion (NO_3^-). An ion is an atom or a collection of atoms that is electrically charged. Ions can be negatively charged (anions) or positively charged (cations). Nitrate ions occur in wetland waters as a result of drainage; they wash in from the surrounding land surfaces, dissolved in the water. Nitrates arise as a result of the decomposition of the dead proteins from plant and animal matter, or from the excreted material of animals. Farmers also spread these chemicals on their land to fertilize the soils and to encourage the growth of their crops, but some of the nitrates applied to the soil are not taken up by the crop; instead they find their way into drainage water and end up in streams, rivers, and wetlands, a process called *eutrophication*. Here plants absorb them and grow faster, but this can lead to problems, as explained in the sidebar.

Calcium is an important element for both plants and animals, but especially for animals that have a bony skeleton

Eutrophication

Nitrogen and phosphorus are two of the most important elements needed for plant growth, so they are major constituents of agricultural fertilizers. These two elements are also found in waste materials, such as sewage, because animals (including humans) filter the excess through their kidneys and excrete it in urine. Industrial processes, particularly detergent use, may also produce waste phosphates. Both nitrates and phosphates are highly soluble and move easily through soils and into water bodies, such as streams and rivers, eventually reaching wetlands.

Aquatic plants, particularly algae, respond very positively to additional fertilizer input because scarcity of these two elements is what often limits their growth. Excessive growth of algae on the surface of water, however, creates conditions that may prove harmful to other plants because the algae form a blanket on the surface that excludes light from the deeper water. As a result, the shaded water plants may die. Even the lower layers of algae eventually die and fall to the bottom of the wetland, where bacteria and fungi begin to decompose them. As the decay process continues, it uses up the available oxygen in the water, and this leads to problems for many animals, which depend on oxygen for their respiration. Some animals, such as water fleas, are very sensitive to low oxygen levels in the water that result from an algal "bloom," and these are lost from the wetland. This type of pollution by excessive fertilization is called *eutrophication,* and it represents a serious threat to many wetland ecosystems.

(including many fish and amphibians) and also those mollusks that have a shell (such as mussels and snails). Calcium comes from the erosion of rocks in the catchment, and the abundance of calcium in water is highly variable, depending on whether there is a lime-rich rock present. The concentration of a chemical in a wetland can be described in a variety of ways, but one simple expression is as parts per million (ppm). Ten thousand parts per million (10,000 ppm) is equivalent to 1 percent. Water that has drained through limestone may have a calcium concentration of around 150 ppm. By comparison, water in an acid lake may have less than one ppm of calcium, while seawater contains more than 400 ppm. In a really saline wetland, such as the Dead Sea in Jordan, the calcium content can be as high as 17,000 ppm, which is 1.7 percent. This great variation in the calcium content of waters has a considerable influence on the types of plants and animals that are found in a wetland.

Phosphorus is another essential element for all living organisms. It is needed for energy storage and exchange in every cell and is also an important component of all the membranes that surround each cell and regulate the movement of other materials both into and out of the cell. In animals with internal skeletons it is also an important component of their bone structure in the form of calcium phosphate. Phosphates, like nitrates, are used in fertilizers and may contribute to the process of eutrophication. They are also used in detergents, so water that drains from household waste may be rich in phosphates. In natural rocks they are quite scarce, so uncontaminated water is not often rich in phosphorus; typical values are 0.01 to 0.05 ppm. But these small quantities of phosphorus are essential to all the living creatures within the wetland.

Sodium and potassium are considerably more common in nature than phosphorus, and animals need both. Potassium is needed for muscle and kidney function in animals, and sodium is required for the activity of nerves. In plants potassium plays an important role in regulating the movement of water between cells, but sodium does not seem to be needed at all. Because sodium is so very common in nature, especially near the sea, plants need to distinguish efficiently between these two very similar elements, selecting the potassium and excluding the sodium. Seawater contains approximately 10,000 ppm (1 percent) sodium and 380 ppm potassium. In locations near the seashore, rain may also be rich in these elements because the seawater is whipped up into the atmosphere by the wind. Freshwater in wetlands from such oceanic sites, such as Nova Scotia, may have concentrations of five ppm sodium and 0.3 ppm potassium. Inland, such as in Wisconsin, the sodium content of freshwater may be only one-tenth of this.

The remaining element of significance is magnesium. This is an important component of the pigment chlorophyll, which green plants need to carry out their photosynthesis. Like sodium, it is abundant in seawater, having a concentration of about 1,300 ppm. It is less common in freshwater, usually composing only 0.5 ppm or less. Together with calcium, magnesium is responsible for the "hardness" of water. This term is most commonly used to describe the difficulty one encounters when trying to use soap to generate lather while washing. Water rich in calcium and magnesium is said to be "hard," and it is difficult to produce soapy bubbles in such a medium. Water poor in calcium and magnesium, on the other hand, is said to be "soft" and is more suitable for washing. Hard water can also generate lime scale in vessels used for boiling water, forming a hard crust over heating elements and often causing failure of the mechanism.

Wetland sediments

As discussed in chapter 1, water can enter a wetland either directly from rainfall, or indirectly from the surrounding landscape, in which case it has passed over or through vegetation, soils, and rocks. Water that comes directly from precipitation may contain some dissolved chemicals (especially in a location close to the sea or to a source of pollution) but contains little particulate matter apart from some dust and pollen that it may have collected on its journey down through the atmosphere. Water that has drained through a landscape, on the other hand, may be rich in particles of eroded rock and may also carry other materials, such as dead plant material, that has been collected in the course of its journey. In an ombrotrophic wetland (one fed solely by rain), therefore, very little particulate matter is brought to the ecosystem from outside, but in a rheotrophic wetland (fed both by rain and drainage water) many types of eroded material may be carried from the catchment into the wetland ecosystem.

Large particles of mineral matter, such as fragments of gravel more than 0.1 inch (2 mm) in diameter, can be swept along only by fast-moving water. Even then, they will not be carried in suspension in the water body, but will bounce along the bed of a river or stream by a process called *saltation*. Once the speed of the moving water slows, which usually takes place when it enters a wetland, the larger particles cease to move as actively and take up a permanent position on the surface of the wetland sediments. Smaller particles, or those that have a lower density and therefore float more easily (such as particles of organic matter, including wood), are carried farther into the wetland. Silt and clay particles, for example, are held in suspension by the moving water, but even they eventually sediment out when the water becomes still, often as a result of the presence of plants growing within the wetland (see "Different kinds of wetlands," pages 10–37).

Microscopic plants and animals inhabit the more gently moving waters of the wetland, floating in the upper layers of the water. Some of these, such as the diatoms, produce shells made of silica called *frustules,* and when these members of the photosynthetic phytoplankton die their frustules sink to the bottom and add to the growing body of sediments. The tiny animals that feed upon the diatoms and other phytoplankton may also have outer coats that are durable and survive after death. Crustaceans, for example, like the water flea daphnia, have outer cases that persist after the animals' death and sink into the sediments. Pollen grains that land on the surface of the water, or are carried by the streams from surrounding areas, lose their cell contents because bacteria in the water consume them, but their outer coats are tough and they too become incorporated in the sediments.

Plant life in the wetland includes many larger forms, the *macrophytes*. Some of these spend their entire lives submerged, while others, the *emergents,* extend above the water surface into the atmosphere. They take root in the sediments at the bottom of the water, and their roots eventually die and form part of the sediment. The leaves, stems, and flowers of these macrophytes also die and sink. Much of this material may become decomposed by bacteria and fungi beneath the water, but some remains and joins the inorganic particles to form sediment. Over time this sediment becomes brown rather than gray in color as organic remains form an increasingly important component. The silts and clays of a young lake give way to the muds of a more mature and productive wetland ecosystem. The process of succession (see "Changing wetlands," pages 37–41) thus leaves a permanent record of its course in the sediments of the wetland. Mineral particles and organic fossils are mixed together in the water and then laid down in a stratified series of layers, year upon year.

In cold climates where the wetland may freeze during the winter and where the soils become more unstable and more easily eroded as snow melts each spring, there may be a distinct rush of eroded mineral particles at the beginning of each year. This produces a band of pale sediment on the bottom of the wetland. During the summer, however, as temperatures rise, plant productivity, including that of phytoplankton, increases, and an organic brown layer is deposited above the pale mineral one. Each year, therefore, is marked by a period of mineral deposition followed by a period of organic deposition, and the sediments that accumulate show clear bands if they are sampled in cross section by excavation or by drilling. These annual bands, resembling the annual growth rings found in the wood of trees, are called *varves,* and they are very useful in allowing wetland scientists to count the number of years back to any particular level in the sediments.

During the course of succession the depth of water decreases as the quantity of sediments builds up. As the water becomes shallower, the contribution of eroded mineral materials from the surrounding catchment declines, while the contribution from the local plant community increases. The result is that the sediments contain an increasing proportion of organic material derived from the dead remains of vegetation. When the sediment contains less than 35 percent of inorganic matter, it is often referred to as peat (see the peat profile on page 54).

Peat is generally rich in the fossil remains of plants and sometimes also animals. It forms as a result of the constant accumulation of dead material on the surface and the failure of the bacteria and fungi to complete the decomposition process and convert all the organic matter back into carbon dioxide as they carry out their respiration. A remnant of dead material therefore builds up year by year. How fast the accumulation takes place depends on two main factors: how fast the litter is being deposited on the surface and how fast the rate of decomposition is proceeding below the surface (see "Decomposition," pages 79–82).

Most of the fossil material in peat is derived from the local vegetation. Plant roots are among the most common types of

Cross section of a peat deposit. This profile shows a blanket mire peat from an island off the coast of Norway, near Bergen. (Courtesy of Peter D. Moore)

fossil because they penetrate down from the surface into the deeper layers of waterlogged sediment where microbial activity is low and decomposition takes place more slowly. Roots, as a consequence, are usually very well preserved. Mosses, particularly the bog moss sphagnum, are an important component of bog peats and are much prized by horticulturalists because of their unusual physical and chemical features (see "Plants of the wetlands," pages 98–105). The leaves, flowers, and fruits of wetland plants can often be found preserved in peat, and these are much more easily identified than roots, so they provide information about the vegetation of the wetland in the past. Microscopic fossils are also present, including the frustules of diatoms, the spores of mosses and ferns, and the pollen grains that fall upon the peat from the local vegetation and from more distant sources.

Animals contribute far less bulk to the wetland ecosystem than do plants (see "Food webs and energy flow," pages 74–79), so it is not surprising that animal remains are less common than plants in the peat deposit. The microscopic remains of small crustaceans can be found, together with the intricately patterned shells of some types of amoeba. These *rhizopods,* or testate amoebae, have a hard shell covering their soft, one-celled bodies, and after the animals' death the shells survive in the peat. The wing cases of beetles are also well preserved in peat because the chitin, the hard substance of which they are composed, is very resistant to decay. These wing cases can appear as good as new, even in peat that is 10,000 years old or more, and experts in beetle identification can determine their precise species.

The remains of vertebrate animals are rare in peat deposits. This is mainly because vertebrate animals are generally far less abundant in a wetland than invertebrates, but is also in part due to poor preservation. Peat deposits, particularly when they have developed into ombrotrophic bogs, tend to be acidic in their chemistry. As a result, any bone material that lies within the peat will dissolve in the course of time. The lime-rich sediments of lakes may contain fossil bones and antlers, but these are rare in peat deposits. If a mammal dies in a peat land environment, then all that is likely to remain a few thousand years later is its skin, fingernails, and hair. In the bogs of northern Europe the bodies of humans have been recovered from many peat deposits. These bodies have often caused great concern to those discovering them because the excellent state of skin preservation may make a 2,000-year-old body look like a recent corpse, prompting a murder inquiry to be undertaken. The bog bodies frequently display evidence of violent death, either by head injuries or by strangulation. The bogs of ancient times were evidently regarded as suitable settings for the disposal of corpses, perhaps intended as offerings to the peat land gods, or perhaps just executed as criminals.

The sediments of wetlands, being stratified in a series of successive layers over the course of time, provide a record of local ecosystem development. Because of the preservation of tiny airborne fossils such as pollen grains, this stratigraphy can also supply information about more widespread change in vegetation, landscape, and human history. Wetland sediments should be regarded as a historical document waiting to be read and interpreted by ecologists, archaeologists, and environmental scientists.

Stories in the sediments

Wetland sediments are a sealed archive, a library of information waiting to be opened and read. The first thing that must be done in order to open the archive is to penetrate the sediments and recover samples of them from different depths. One approach to this is excavation. Archaeologists faced with the problem of delving through buried layers usually dig trenches in selected positions so that they can obtain a cross section of the deposits. Then they may strip areas of their soil, layer by layer, as they penetrate to older materials. Those who wish to study wetland stratigraphy can adopt the same approach, but it does result in the damage or even destruction of the site, and many wetlands are of too great conservation interest to allow this to happen. There is also the practical difficulty of removing excess water from the site; any open trench will soon fill with water and become unworkable, so wetland archaeologists have to be well supplied with pumps.

An alternative approach is to drill through the sediments using various kinds of coring devices. Most wetland sediments are reasonably soft, so it is often possible to recover a core by hand, using a sampling chamber and a series of extension rods. The chamber, usually shaped like a cylindrical rocket with a pointed tip, is forced down into the sediment either from the surface of the peat land, if it is firm enough to hold the people conducting the research, or from a platform or a boat if the surface is water-covered or very soft. Some researchers prefer to sample lakes in the depths of winter when they can take cores through ice. The sample chamber is forced to the required depth in the sediment and is then opened to take a core of the sediment. When it is returned to the surface, the core is then extracted, wrapped, and returned to the laboratory for physical, chemical, and biological analysis. In this way a record of the sediment history can be obtained with minimum damage to the site.

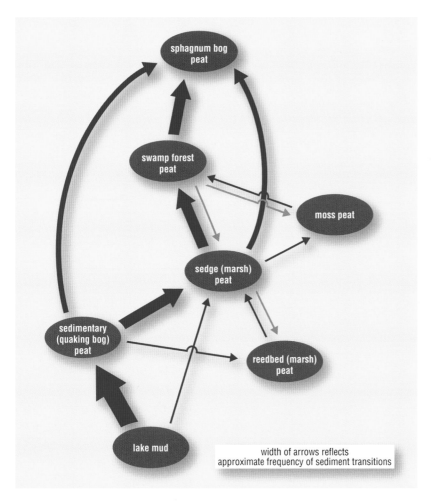

width of arrows reflects approximate frequency of sediment transitions

The most common sequences of wetland sediments in North American wetlands (based on the work of John Tallis)

The sequence of sediment types and their contained fossils provides a detailed record of how a particular wetland developed and enables the scientist to reconstruct the course of succession at that site. The general course of wetland succession described in chapter 1 (see "Changing wetlands," pages 37–41) is typical of a temperate wetland site, but extensive stratigraphic research in a wide range of wetlands shows that many variations on the general theme are possible. The illustration on page 57 is based on a summary of published research on wetland stratigraphy, and it gives a general survey of the characteristic successional sequences that have been described in temperate North American wetlands. The wide arrows show the most commonly found pathways of development, and the narrow arrows show less frequent developmental tracks. The red arrows show that reversals in the expected direction of wetland development can occasionally take place.

The diagram reveals some general trends in wetland development:

1. Wetlands tend to develop from aquatic conditions to increasingly dry conditions often dominated by trees. This process is called *terrestrialization*.
2. Wetland forests (swamps) frequently become invaded by bog mosses, which act like a sponge and create increasingly wet conditions once more. This process is called *paludification*.
3. Wetlands very rarely develop into dry forest. Only a change in the drainage pattern of a catchment can lead to this outcome.

The microscopic fossils in the sediments can provide additional information about the changing conditions as the succession proceeds. The diatoms, for example, whose past presence is recorded by their shells, or frustules, in the sediments, can tell us about the chemical conditions in the wetland at any given time. Some diatoms prefer acidic conditions, while others are found only in lime-rich waters; some perform best when the water contains abundant nitrates, while others prefer water that has very low fertility. The stratified remains of the diatom frustules contain a complete record of the changing diatom communities in the past, and from these one can deduce the chemical conditions of those times. The evidence from diatoms has proved particularly helpful when analysts are trying to trace the development and the causes of modern pollution problems. In Lake Washington, near Seattle, for example, there are concerns about increasing fertility of the waters resulting from eutrophication (see the sidebar on page 49). In order to trace the history of this process, scientists extracted the diatom frustules from the upper layers of the sediments of the lake and were able to show that there was a sudden increase in abundance of those diatoms preferring nutrient-rich conditions at about 1850, when the city of Seattle began to expand. The changes in the lake are therefore clearly linked to human activities in the area, such as farming, sewage treatment, and waste disposal.

Another problem for wetlands is the increasing acidity of rainfall. The changing acidity of lakes can be traced in the diatom fossils, and in this way aquatic scientists have deduced past pH fluctuations in the lakes of Scotland. Below 20 inches (50 cm) in the sediments of one lake in southern Scotland, the diatoms consisted of species that prefer neutral or slightly alkaline water, while above that level species that prefer acid conditions became increasingly abundant. The critical horizon was dated to 1900, and the acidification is thought related to atmospheric pollution from an electricity-generating power station nearby.

Pollen grains in sediments (see the sidebar on page 60) provide evidence of the vegetation in past times. The interpretation of fossil pollen grains is fraught with difficulties, but these tiny fossils can reveal much about past landscapes and changing conditions.

The results obtained from pollen analysis of lake sediments or peat deposits are presented in the form of a pollen diagram, like the one shown on page 61. The vertical axis represents depth of sediment, which is related to its age. This particular diagram shows the dates of the different layers of sediment. The abundance of pollen of different types is represented by the vertical curves, illustrating the changing fortunes of various plants over the course of time. In

Pollen grains

Flowering plants and conifers produce pollen grains as a means of carrying the male gamete (reproductive cell) from the male reproductive organ to the female. The main transport mechanisms are the wind or an animal, most frequently an insect. The pollen grain must be small so that it can remain suspended in air or attached to an insect's body, and it must be produced in large numbers, especially if carried by the wind, which is a distinctly random and chancy way to make contact with the female gamete. The reproductive cells are delicate and need to be protected on their journey, which means that they require a very tough outer wall. This has to be robust enough to withstand desiccation, yet flexible enough to allow the cells to expand and contract as they take up or lose water. Pollen grains possess such a coat, which is made of a very strong material called *sporopollenin*. Pollen grains are produced in such large numbers and are scattered so widely into the atmosphere (especially those using wind transport) that many of them fall to the ground or onto the surface of water. The latter may become incorporated into the sediments of lakes or peat lands, and although the delicate inner cells are quickly consumed by fungi and bacteria, the outer coats may be preserved for thousands or even millions of years.

Fortunately for wetland ecologists, different plant types produce distinctive pollen grains. The outer coat varies in the number of pores it contains and also in the type of sculpturing on its surface. Consequently, it is possible to identify fossil pollen grains with a certain degree of confidence. Some plants can even be identified to the level of species on the basis of their pollen grains, but others are not quite so distinctive. Grasses, for example, cannot be determined beyond the family level, and some trees, such as oak, are very difficult to identify to species level with any degree of precision. But the fossil pollen grains can still provide a picture of the vegetation surrounding a wetland in past times. The technique of pollen analysis of sediments has provided a wealth of information about the evolution of the Earth's vegetation and landscape.

this case just three tree types (beech, oak, and pine) and three types of herbaceous plants (grasses, ragweed, and sorrel) are shown. A full pollen diagram would contain dozens of pollen types and depict much more detail than this generalized and simplified version.

Since 1200 C.E. there have been some considerable changes in the composition of the forest, shifting from beech to oak and pine, and then becoming much more open with more

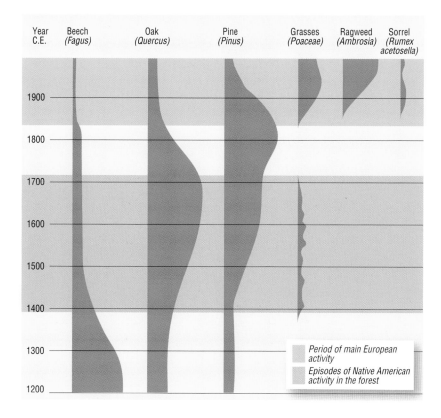

| Year C.E. | Beech (Fagus) | Oak (Quercus) | Pine (Pinus) | Grasses (Poaceae) | Ragweed (Ambrosia) | Sorrel (Rumex acetosella) |

Period of main European activity

Episodes of Native American activity in the forest

Typical pollen profile from a North American (New England) wetland. The vertical axis corresponds to the sediment depth (and therefore the age), and the thickness of the curves represents the proportional abundance of each pollen type. Two periods of human activity are recorded, one corresponding to Native American settlement and the second showing the vegetation response to the arrival of European settlers.

grasses and herbs. The rise in pine in New England is associated with the activities of Native American populations, who used fire to modify their environment and supplied conditions under which pine has great advantages over other trees, because pine is very fire resistant. The really intensive changes, however, occurred with the settlement of European immigrants, who cleared the forest for more extensive agriculture and produced a landscape in which grasses and herbs (including ragweed) flourished.

The technique of pollen analysis has proved extremely valuable in supplying a picture of the changing forests and landscapes that surrounded wetlands. By analyzing sediments from ancient lakes, we can piece together an understanding of the way forests responded to the end of the Ice Age around 12,000 years ago. In New England, for example, spruce was an early invader as conditions became warmer, while beech was later in expanding its populations at around 8,000 years ago. Hickory was later still, only attaining importance in the area some 5,000 years ago. By studying pollen sequences in wetlands over the entire country, scientists have even been able to trace the locations in which different trees survived the Ice Age and the routes along which they have spread as conditions became warmer. Using pollen analysis, we can also reconstruct the vegetation that existed before humans, particularly the pioneers from Europe, first arrived on the scene.

Similar work has been conducted in wetlands over the entire world, allowing pollen analysts to show how vegetation responds to climate change and how human cultures have had an effect on their environment. Using pollen analysis, it has been possible to investigate such questions as how the tropical rain forest responded to the cold that resulted in the glaciation of the temperate zone, how agriculture spread and resulted in extensive changes in natural habitats, and how the deserts have changed their extent during the course of time. Wetlands contain an extremely large reservoir of such information, most of which has yet to be unveiled.

Dating the sediments

Whether the subject of study is the development of individual wetlands through the record of their sediments or wider questions of environmental change, there must be a secure system of dating the stratified sequences so that the changes observed can be assigned to a particular time frame. In lake sediments, if there are strong temperature differences between seasons and if the conditions within the lake are very stable so that sediment resuspension and mixing does not occur, then annual bands or *varves* are formed. Dating such sediments simply involves counting the number of varves back from the present surface.

Even in the absence of varves, or in peat deposits where annual layering does not occur, it is sometimes possible to detect a particular horizon that can be firmly dated. One of the most reliable of such horizons is produced by a layer of *tephra,* or volcanic ash, that is derived from a volcanic eruption and can be spread through the atmosphere over a radius of thousands of miles. Tephra deposits in wetlands take the form of tiny glasslike particles that are clearly visible under a microscope. One remarkable feature of tephra is that the chemistry of the particles allows them to be identified with a particular volcano and, indeed, with a specific eruption. Once this is known, it is possible to date a tephra layer with a high degree of precision.

One of the most widely used methods of dating is radiocarbon analysis. This method relies on the fact that cosmic rays are constantly causing changes in the atoms that they encounter in the outer atmosphere. Carbon normally has an atomic weight of 12, but cosmic ray impacts can generate a carbon atom with a weight of 14. Over the course of time, radioactive ^{14}C (pronounced "carbon 14") decays to produce ^{12}C ("carbon 12"), but this is quite a slow process. It takes more than 5,500 years for half of the ^{14}C atoms in any population to decay. This is called its half-life. When plants take up carbon as carbon dioxide and incorporate it into their tissues, they do not distinguish between the two types, so the dead plant material that enters the peat contains some ^{14}C. As time goes by and the radioactive form decays, the abundance of ^{14}C in relation to ^{12}C becomes smaller. Because the decay rate is a known constant, it is possible to calculate how long ago the peat was formed. The quantity of ^{14}C in a sample is measured using an atomic mass spectrometer, and from this analysts can estimate the date of origin of the plant or animal material. There is a complication, however, because the rate at which ^{14}C has been formed in the upper atmosphere over the course of time has not been constant. This means that the apparent radiocarbon age does not correspond precisely with the actual (sometimes called solar) age. Fortunately, this has not proved a serious problem. It has been possible to radiocarbon date materials of known age (such as the wood from particular growth rings of ancient or fossil trees) and thus to correlate radiocarbon years with solar years. The relatively short half-life of ^{14}C does mean that material dating from about 40,000 years or more ago contains so little of the heavy isotope that it is difficult to measure its concentration accurately. So the radiocarbon dating method is suitable only for samples from the late part of the last glaciation or more recently. However, this time frame encompasses the age of most modern wetlands.

Geology of the ancient wetlands

Wetlands are not a new ecosystem on this planet. Their history is almost as old as that of life itself. Some of the earliest records of living creatures on the Earth come from ancient sediments of coastal wetlands. Cells of primitive bacteria and algae are found in lumps of rock called *stromatolites* that had built up in shallow coastal regions from the accretion of lime and silica. Some of these stromatolites are believed to be more than 3 billion years old. The wetlands played an important part in the colonization of the land by living organisms in Devonian times (408 million to 360 million years ago) because the first plants and animals to emerge from the oceans were still very dependent on water for their life cycles. Algae, liverworts, mosses, and ferns all need water in order to reproduce, so they would have grown in and around the early wetlands.

The most ancient of the peat-forming wetlands are also Devonian in age. Their fossil remains are found widely scattered in West Virginia, Belgium, and Siberia. They were dominated by early relatives of the ferns. Peat-forming wetlands became abundant in Carboniferous times (360 million to 290 million years ago). In these times tropical swamps, dominated by tall trees that were related to modern ferns and horsetails, built up deep deposits of peat. It is important to remember that the continents were in very different positions around 300 million years ago. Much of what is now North America and Europe lay in the equatorial regions of the Earth, which is why they contain the fossil remains of these ancient tropical swamps. The peat of 300 million years ago has subsequently become buried and compacted so that it is now a hard rock, coal, but just like modern peat it has a very high proportion of organic material within it, so that it can be combusted to provide energy. This fossil fuel is the product of the ancient peat lands.

The map shows the distribution of coal deposits around the world, but these were laid down at different times in the Earth's history. The Devonian and Carboniferous coals have already been mentioned, but there were also coal-forming swamps in the subsequent Jurassic Period (208 million to 145 million years ago), most notably in Australia. It was at this

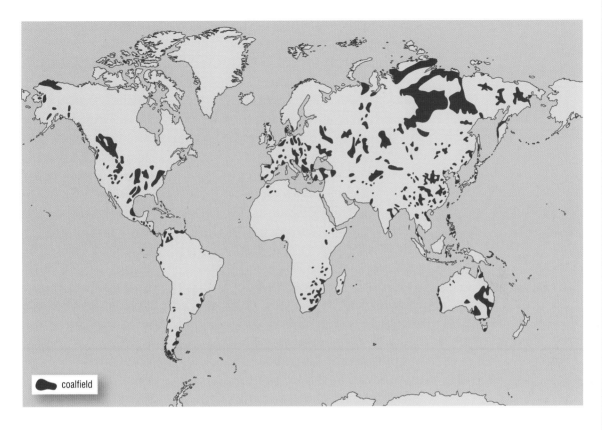

coalfield

time that the coniferous trees were becoming more abundant over the face of the Earth, and by the Cretaceous Period (145 million to 65 million years ago) many of the coal swamps were dominated by relatives of the swamp cypress, now found in the Florida Everglades. For an impression of what the coal-forming swamps of the age of dinosaurs looked like, the Everglades are difficult to improve upon. Some of the coal deposits of central Europe and China are even more recent in origin. Many of these recently formed coals are not as hard and compacted as the more ancient ones. They are sometimes referred to as brown coal.

Coal varies in its properties and its quality as a fuel. A high-grade coal, such as anthracite, is predominantly made up of organic materials with very little inorganic content. This means that when it is burned there is very little ash left at the end of the process. This fact helps us to understand the conditions under which such a coal was formed. We know that modern peat with low mineral ash content can accumulate

Distribution of the major coal deposits of the world

only under ombrotrophic conditions, where there is no inflow of drainage water carrying silts and clays. We must conclude, therefore, that the ancient coal-forming peat lands resembled modern raised bogs in having extensive domes of peat, the surface of which was elevated above the flow of groundwater and was fed only by rain. It is difficult to imagine these huge tropical forested bogs accumulating deep peat deposits in the form of extensive domes over the landscape. It is also difficult to explain how deep deposits of peat could accumulate. Modern bogs rarely exceed 40 feet (13 m) in depth, and that is before any compression and compaction of the deposits. The ancient peat bogs were formed in regions where the Earth's crust was sinking, so that as they grew, the sea level in the surrounding estuaries continued to rise. Bogs were probably swamped by rising oceans and then began their growth over again, producing organic coals alternating with inorganic layers produced by the rising sea. Coal deposits are often stacked in this way.

The natural world has influenced the cultural development and the history of humanity. It is important to remember that without the accumulation of solar energy in the peat deposits of these ancient wetlands there may have been no industrial revolution. The world today would have been a very different place.

Conclusions

Wetlands fit into the landscape in different ways. If the precipitation is very high, then wetlands may be found almost anywhere in a landscape, even on ridges and slopes, but usually the wetlands are found in the hollows and valleys on impermeable rocks, where water naturally accumulates (topogenous wetlands). Some wetlands occur where impermeable rocks underlie porous rocks and where water comes to the surface of the ground in springs; these are soligenous wetlands.

The chemistry of wetland water is strongly affected by the rocks through which it has passed. Rainwater is generally slightly acid and poor in nutrient elements unless the ocean is close by, in which case calcium, sodium, and magnesium are usually abundant. Water that has passed through limestone is rich is calcium, but water from acid rocks, such as granite or sandstone, is generally poor in calcium. Nitrates and phosphates are particularly associated with human activities (farming, industry, sewage, and waste disposal). Their presence may stimulate plant growth, but it can lead to eutrophication and oxygen depletion.

The sediments of wetlands contain both inorganic and organic materials. The early stages in wetland succession usually produce predominantly inorganic sediments, and the organic content increases in the course of succession. Fossils within the sediments provide evidence of the course of development in a wetland so that the direction succession has taken can be reconstructed. Some microscopic fossils, such as pollen grains, supply information about the changing vegetation and environmental conditions over a wide area. Wetland sediments are thus an archive of historical information. Interpretation of this information requires accurate dating of sediment horizons, but techniques are available to achieve this, particularly radiocarbon dating.

Some wetlands are particularly ancient and provide information about the evolution and development of living organisms and ecosystems. The storage of energy in the organic remains of these ancient peat lands has had a profound effect on the development of human culture, supplying a basis for the industrial revolution.

CHAPTER 3

THE WETLAND ECOSYSTEM

Every single organism on the Earth interacts with its surroundings. Other members of the same species often compose part of its surroundings, so that the organism, especially if it is a relatively advanced animal, will have social interactions with its peers. A collection of individuals of the same species interacting in this way is called a *population*. An organism will also interact with other living creatures belonging to different species. Some of these may be its prey, while others may be its predators; some will be harmful parasites, while others compete with it for the same food resources. A collection of different species living together and interacting in all these different ways is called a *community*. Then, finally, this collection of living organisms coexisting in a community will be interacting with the nonliving world that forms a setting for all life. Plants are rooted in the soil, from which they absorb the minerals they need to grow, and they take up carbon dioxide gas from the atmosphere, which they convert into sugars in the process of photosynthesis. Animals also drink water and supplement their minerals in this way; some may even eat soil if they run short of certain elements. Taken as a whole, a community of different species of animals and plants living in the physical and chemical setting of the nonliving world, is called an *ecosystem*.

What is an ecosystem?

The concept of an ecosystem is an extremely useful one to ecologists and conservationists. It is an approach to the study of the natural world that can be applied at a range of different scales. One could take a single rotting log in a forest and regard it as an ecosystem, studying the way in which the energy and mineral elements contained in the dead wood are decomposed by fungi and bacteria, which are then eaten by invertebrate animals, which in turn may be fed upon by carnivorous beetles, which attract visiting woodpeckers that take the energy contained in the beetle out of that particular ecosystem and into another. On the other hand, one could regard the entire forest as an ecosystem, in which case the fallen logs are simply a part of a greater whole in which the photosynthesis of the trees is trapping the energy of sunlight, storing it in wood, and eventually providing an energy source for the microbes and animals inhabiting the decomposing materials of the forest floor. The woodpecker is now part of the same ecosystem, performing its own part in the organization of the whole.

Although we can use the ecosystem idea at many different scales, all ecosystems have certain features in common. All ecosystems have a flow of energy through them. The source of energy for most ecosystems is sunlight, which is made available to living organisms by photosynthesis conducted by green plants. There are some bacteria that photosynthesize, and there are some that obtain energy from nonsolar sources, such as chemical reactions with inorganic materials (for instance, the oxidation of iron), but these are of little significance in most ecosystems when compared with the contribution of green plant photosynthesis. Some ecosystems, such as the rotting log in the forest or a mudflat in the estuary of a river, import energy from other ecosystems. Dead plant materials, rich in the energy derived ultimately from sunlight, are brought into these ecosystems and supply the needs of the animals and microbes that feed upon them. In this flow of energy through an ecosystem we can distinguish groups of organisms with different roles to play. The plants are primary producers, fixing solar energy into organic matter; they are said to be autotrophic in their nutrition, which literally means that they can feed themselves. Herbivores are primary consumers; they are dependent on plants for energy, so they are said to be heterotrophic, meaning that they need to be fed by others. Predatory animals are also heterotrophic. They too depend ultimately on plants, but indirectly because they feed upon the herbivores or upon the animals that eat herbivores. These are secondary and tertiary consumers.

They occupy different positions in a hierarchy of feeding, sometimes referred to as a *food web* in the ecosystem. Meanwhile, the waste material produced by living organisms and the dead parts or dead bodies of those organisms that escape consumption by predators and survive long enough to die a natural death are used by the decomposer organisms. Detritivorous animals may eat some of these materials and derive energy from them, but ultimately the decomposers in the ecosystem consist of the bacteria and fungi, which use up all the energy-rich materials that remain. Nothing is wasted, nothing is lost. All the energy entering the ecosystem is finally used up and is dissipated as heat in the course of *respiration,* a process in which the stored energy is released as work is performed.

While energy flows through the ecosystem, chemical elements are cycled. Carbon atoms, for example, that are taken up by plants in a gaseous form, carbon dioxide, are incorporated into carbohydrates and may be stored in this form or as fats, or may be converted to proteins by the addition of the element nitrogen (derived from the soil), or perhaps converted into other compounds by the addition of other elements, such as phosphorus to make phospholipids. The materials built into plant bodies are consumed by animals, and a proportion passes through the body of the consumer to be voided as waste. Respiration results in the release of carbon back into the atmosphere as carbon dioxide gas, while the nitrogen and phosphorus, together with other elements, are released back into the soil in the process of decomposition. They are recycled and can be used over and over again. Energy passes once through the ecosystem and is finally dissipated, but chemical elements may cycle round and round the ecosystem indefinitely. The constantly turning wheel of element motion is called a *nutrient cycle.*

In addition to the cycle of nutrients, however, there is also usually an import and export of elements to an ecosystem. A stream entering an ecosystem will bring dissolved minerals from the ecosystems in the catchment area. Rainfall will also bring a supply of elements, its richness depending on how close the site is to the ocean. Animals may migrate into an ecosystem and bring elements from outside, such as the salmon that migrate up rivers, where they breed and die, bringing elements that they have collected in their ocean feeding grounds. Plant materials, including twigs and leaves, may be washed or blown into a pond, supplying a source of elements from another ecosystem. But just as these processes bring elements into an ecosystem, they also take them out. Streams may leave an ecosystem, animals move out, and plant material may be blown away. So when studying an ecosystem, one must consider the imports and exports in order to understand the balance of supply and loss in both energy and mineral elements.

How do wetlands work?

As chapter 1 demonstrated, there are many different types of wetland. Each of these can be considered as an ecosystem, with its own particular pattern of energy flow and nutrient cycle. There are, however, certain features that wetlands all have in common and that make them different from most other ecosystems. The most obvious feature is their wetness, which leads to unusual patterns of energy flow and storage. The main problem that water presents is the low availability of oxygen that often results. All living organisms (with the exception of some very specialized fungi and bacteria) need a supply of oxygen so that they can respire. The energy present in the organic compounds they consume can be tapped only if oxygen is available so that the carbon from sugars and other sources can be converted into carbon dioxide. Oxygen is readily available in air because it composes about 21 percent of the atmosphere, but under water oxygen becomes less easily available. Oxygen dissolves in water, and fast-flowing waters may be rich in dissolved oxygen, but when the water is still, oxygen movement is dependent on the process of diffusion. Diffusion is a kind of migration of molecules from areas of high density to areas of low density. Oxygen moves gradually from the surface layers, where the water is in contact with air, down into the deeper layers, where oxygen is being consumed by the decomposers in the mud at the bottom of the wetland. But for a dissolved oxygen molecule, moving through water is rather like a person trying to wade through molasses. In water oxygen diffuses 10,000 times more slowly than it does in air, so as oxygen is consumed by the respiration of organisms in stagnant water, it is replaced only very slowly.

The most serious consequence of the slow diffusion of dissolved oxygen in water is that the decomposition of dead organic matter may be incomplete. In most ecosystems all of the residual organic matter that falls to the floor and enters the soil is eventually decomposed and is lost, but in wetlands the slow decomposition may lead to an imbalance in the flow of energy, resulting in some energy-rich organic matter becoming permanently stored in the sediments of the ecosystem. It is this growing reservoir of organic carbon that has resulted in the formation of coal in the ancient wetlands and that leads to the buildup of mud and peat in many modern wetlands. Because of this imbalance, wetlands act as a "sink" or storehouse for atmospheric carbon and help in the absorption of the current excessive release of carbon by human beings through the combustion of fossil fuels (see "Wetlands as carbon sinks," pages 160–162). As the wetland develops through the process of succession (see "Changing wetlands," pages 37–41), the energy reservoir in the sediments becomes bigger, and this is the cause of the growing mass of peat that we find in the raised bogs of the temperate zone and the extensive tropical forested bogs of Southeast Asia.

The pattern of energy flow through a wetland ecosystem is shown in the illustration. As can be seen, the movement through producers, consumers, and decomposers follows the expected sequence that is found in all ecosystems, but some of the energy moving through this system remains stored in the organic matter of the sediments.

In addition to the unusual pattern of energy flow in wetlands, the nutrient cycling patterns are also distinctive. As noted previously, there are two main types of wetland, which differ in their pattern of water input (see "Wetland distribution in the landscape," pages 7–10). Rheotrophic wetlands receive water from both the precipitation that falls from the sky and also from groundwater inputs coming from springs, soil drainage, streams, and rivers. Ombrotrophic wetlands, on the other hand, receive their water only from rainfall. The

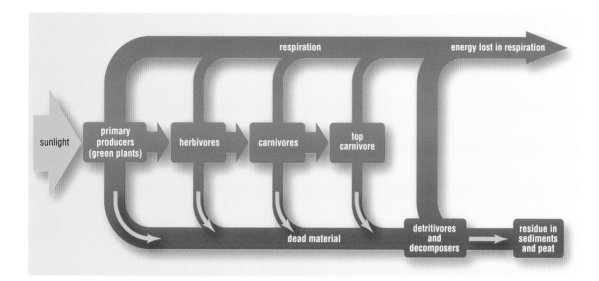

nature of the nutrient cycle of a wetland will vary according to which of these types of hydrology is operating. Ombrotrophic wetlands will generally receive far less input of nutrients than do rheotrophic ones, although an ombrotrophic ecosystem close to the ocean may be relatively rich, while a rheotrophic one that lies on acid, nutrient-poor bedrock may be relatively poor in nutrients. In most cases an ombrotrophic wetland will have an impoverished nutrient cycle compared to that of a rheotrophic one.

Almost all wetlands begin their successional development as rheotrophic, flow-fed systems, and the inflowing streams bring suspended inorganic materials into the ecosystem. These accumulate in the sediments of the wetland and add to the organic matter that accumulates there, gradually raising the level of the growing deposits relative to the water level. These materials can be regarded as a nutrient reservoir that becomes fossilized in the sediments. Plant roots may tap into this reservoir, but most of the chemicals that come to rest in the wetland sediments remain there until some catastrophe leads to the drainage or destruction of the entire ecosystem. The growing deposits of sediment beneath the surface of wetlands, therefore, form a reservoir of both energy and nutrients. In this respect, wetlands differ from all other ecosystems.

The pattern of energy flow in a wetland ecosystem

Food webs and energy flow

We have seen that energy flows through an ecosystem in one direction, but there are many paths along which it may pass. It is very rare in nature for energy to move through an ecosystem in a simple direct path. A free-floating producer, such as a single-celled alga, may be eaten by a microscopic crustacean that is then consumed by a fish that is eaten by a heron. This may seem like a simple, linear food chain, but when the heron dies and falls into the water, it will be invaded by fly larvae that may be eaten by other fish, which are consumed by an otter. So some of the energy has moved off into another path and will take longer before it is eventually released in respiration. Energy does not cycle, but it often takes a complicated route through an ecosystem before it is finally dissipated. Ecologists therefore prefer to use the term *food webs* rather than *food chains* to describe the flow of energy in natural ecosystems.

Simplified food web from a temperate, shallow, still pool wetland

The first diagram shows a simplified food web for a temperate open-water wetland. It is simplified in the sense that some groups of organisms, such as insect larvae and mol-

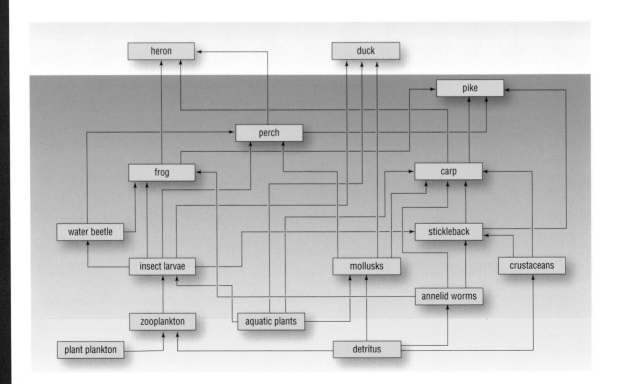

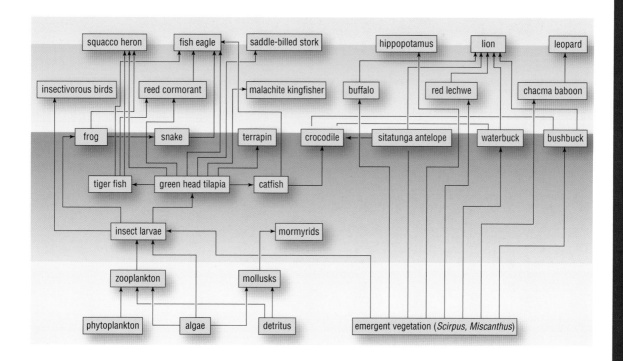

lusks, are considered as a group, whereas there is actually a range of possible feeding activities within these categories. Mollusks, for example, include bivalves such as freshwater mussels, which live in the mud and filter microscopic food from the water, and also snails, which graze over the surface of stones or on emergent plants. Even in a simplified form, however, it is apparent that there are many possible routes along which energy flows in this ecosystem.

The second diagram shows the food web of a tropical swamp, the Okavango Delta in southern Africa. This scheme is also simplified, but it shows the considerable range of diversity that exists in this tropical wetland. Mammals, birds, reptiles, and amphibians are all more diverse than in the temperate ecosystem, and this is generally true of tropical sites. It is not clear why tropical ecosystems have a higher biodiversity than temperate ones, but ecologists and biogeographers have made many attempts to account for the observation. One likely contributing factor is the greater primary productivity of the tropical sites. If more energy is being trapped and stored by the ecosystem, then it is reasonable to suppose that it can then support a greater variety of wildlife.

Simplified food web from a tropical marsh. This example is based on the Okavango Swamp in southern Africa.

The favorable climate, with no occurrence of frost to disrupt the life of the swamp, may also encourage a high diversity, although the Okavango Delta does experience regular drought, which creates a serious problem for the survival of aquatic animals and plants. The Tropics are also thought to be a center of evolution, so the richness of the equatorial region may reflect the rate at which new species have been generated in this part of the world.

Whatever the cause of tropical biodiversity, the fact is undeniable. The existence of such richness gives rise to another question—whether high levels of diversity make an ecosystem more stable. Stability in an ecosystem means that it is resistant to disturbance, and that when it is damaged it rapidly repairs itself and returns to its former state. Once again, ecologists are not entirely in agreement about the relationship between diversity and stability. It is reasonable to expect that high diversity would render an ecosystem more stable because there are more species present to fill any gaps resulting from a catastrophe. Suppose, for example, that one species of fish became infected by a disease and was lost to the ecosystem. The abundance of fish species within the ecosystem would mean that the predators of the lost fish would have alternative prey. There would be an adjustment to the food web, and the overall disruption would be minimal. If there were few species of fish, however, as is the case in most temperate wetlands, then the loss of one species could have serious repercussions on the entire food web of the ecosystem.

The ombrotrophic bogs of the temperate zone are generally low in biodiversity, so their food webs are simpler than those of tropical swamps. Generally, these acidic, nutrient-poor habitats have low primary productivity, which may be the cause of their low biodiversity. The table compares the primary productivity of a range of wetland types from around the world. The Arctic wetlands have the lowest productivity overall, mainly because their growing season is so short and temperatures are low even in summer. Among the temperate wetlands there is a great range in productivity, from the low levels of the raised bogs to the high productiv-

Primary productivity values for a range of wetlands

Wetland	Net primary productivity*
Arctic sedge marshes	0.26–0.80 (0.1–0.3)
Temperate raised bogs	0.80–1.85 (0.3–0.7)
Temperate sedge marshes	1.32–2.64 (0.5–1.0)
Temperate forested swamps	1.06–3.17 (0.4–1.2)
Temperate reed and cattail marshes	1.32–6.60 (0.5–2.5)
Tropical papyrus swamps	5.28–26.40 (2–10)

*Weights are in pounds per square yard per year (figures in brackets are in kilograms per square meter per year) in dry weight.

ity of temperate marshes, particularly the reed and cattail marshes. The degree of productivity is closely related to the supply of nutrients, the rheotrophic wetlands being richer in nutrients and higher in productivity than the ombrotrophic ones. As can be seen, the tropical swamps are extremely productive, ranking among the most productive ecosystems on Earth. The productivity does vary, however, according to the nutrient supply available to the individual swamp. A rich supply of nutrients (particularly nitrogen, phosphorus, and potassium) ensures high productivity.

Energy passes through the ecosystem, proceeding from plant to animal and from one animal to another, and at each stage some of the energy is lost. When an herbivore consumes some of the primary production, a proportion of the energy contained within the plant material is absorbed by the animal and becomes incorporated into the animal's body. But much of the plant matter passes through the gut of the consumer and is voided as feces, so the grazing animal is not 100 percent efficient in its treatment and transfer of the plant's energy. Similarly, when a predator kills and eats its prey, only a proportion of the energy contained in the prey animal actually becomes part of the predator's body. The precise efficiency varies depending upon the stage in the energy transfer through the ecosystem and the animals involved in the interaction, but measurements in aquatic ecosystems suggest that about 10 percent of the energy present at one feeding level (called a *trophic level*) is passed on to the next level. The remainder passes to detritivores and decomposers. This gives some indication of how little each consumer receives of the amount of energy that is consumed.

One consequence of the inefficiency of energy transfer in ecosystems is that the amount of energy available gradually decreases as it moves up from one trophic level to the next. There is a larger quantity (biomass) of vegetation in a cattail marsh, for example, than there is of herbivores. Similarly, if one could gather together all the herbivores in the marsh, from caterpillars to deer, their combined mass would be several times greater than that of their predators. The loss of about 90 percent of the energy at each stage of transfer means that the biomass present within each trophic level declines with each step up the food web. By the time these resources reach the top predator level (in a cattail marsh this may be a peregrine falcon or an alligator), there is only a very small quantity present per unit area of the marsh. This arrangement is known as a *pyramid of biomass*. The energy pyramid is broad at the base, supported by the mass of vegetation, and becomes smaller at each trophic level until the top predators occupy the small biomass supported at the summit. This energy structure is common to most terrestrial ecosystems, including the wetlands, and renders them stable.

Certain types of wetland ecosystems, however, do not obey the normal rules. The open-water aquatic stages in the wetland succession may have an inverted pyramid of biomass. In a pool that lacks any large aquatic plants, the primary production is carried out by microscopic algae, the phytoplankton. These are consumed by zooplankton (microscopic animals), which are then eaten by insect predators and fish. If we were to collect and weigh each of these trophic levels, we would probably find that the fish biomass was greater than the zooplankton biomass, and that the zooplankton outweighed the phytoplankton. So the pyramid of biomass is inverted. Nevertheless, the system remains stable. The reason for the stability is that the one-celled phytoplankton reproduces at a very high rate. The cells are constantly dividing and replicating, replacing the cells that are being consumed by the zooplankton. The small size and the fast reproduction make up for the small total biomass of primary producers present at any given time. In most wetland ecosystems, however, the primary producer biomass is high and the pyramid of biomass model applies.

One other consequence of the energy loss that occurs at each transfer between trophic levels is that there is a limit to the number of trophic levels that can be supported in any ecosystem. A chain of transfer involving more than five or six levels is very unusual. Consider an example in which a wetland plant is eaten by a caterpillar, which is food for a beetle, which is eaten by a shrew, which falls prey to a red-tailed hawk. There are five levels in this chain, involving four energy transfers. Because most of the energy is lost at each transfer, little remains to support further transfers at even higher levels. Feeding chains are thus limited by the behavior of energy as it flows through an ecosystem, and the complexity of food webs is also limited by the amount of energy supplied by the primary producers at the base of the system.

Decomposition

As has been explained, wetlands are extremely unusual ecosystems in that they contain a growing reservoir of organic material in their sediments. Although some of this may be imported from outside the ecosystem and brought in by tributary rivers and streams, much of the organic detritus (sometimes all of it) is produced within the ecosystem. This means that energy is being fixed by photosynthesis faster than it can be released in respiration by the living organisms of the ecosystem (including the microbes). Some wetland ecosystems have very high productivity, such as the papyrus swamps of the Tropics, but these are not the wetlands with the highest rates of organic matter retention. Raised bogs are one of the most effective wetlands at building a store of peat, often achieving a growth of an inch (25 mm) every 25 years. This may not seem very much, but when it accumulates over areas of several square miles it can represent a lot of stored carbon. Raised bogs, as can be seen in the table on page 77, are among the lowest ranking of the wetlands in terms of productivity, yet are among the highest when it comes to carbon storage. So the key to understanding the accumulation of organic matter in wetlands lies in the low rate of decomposition, not in the productivity.

Waterlogging and poor oxygen diffusion under water are evidently major factors in controlling the rate of decomposition, but there are other factors as well. Some materials are less palatable to bacteria and fungi than others. The bog mosses (genus *Sphagnum*) produce compounds called *polyphenols* that are resistant to microbial attack. High levels of acidity, low nutrient availability, and low temperatures on the northern peat lands also reduce the level of microbial activity and lead to peat accumulation.

Water saturation, however, remains the most important consideration, as can be demonstrated by a simple experiment, first conducted on a bog in England. The experiment consists of taking samples of bog moss, enclosing them in fine muslin bags so that decomposer organisms can penetrate but the mosses cannot fall out, and burying them in the bog peat at different depths. After a period of three months in the summer, the samples buried within eight inches (20 cm) of the bog surface will have lost between 5 and 10 percent of their weight; decomposition has been relatively rapid. But samples below eight inches are found to have lost much less weight, usually less than 1 percent, and this applies to samples at virtually any greater depth in the peat profile. The conclusion is that decomposition takes place mainly in the upper few inches of the peat and continues at a very low rate farther down the profile.

In order to explain the reason for this pattern in decomposition, another experiment is required. In it a polished silver wire is pushed down into the peat and left there for a few minutes. Upon being withdrawn, the lower part of the wire, beneath a depth of about eight inches, will be coated with a black layer, while the upper part remains shiny. The black deposit is silver sulfide. Its presence on the wire means that the lower part of the peat contains little oxygen and that any sulfur derived from organic matter is in the sulfide form; if oxygen is present, it becomes oxidized to sulfate. The sulfide may be combined with hydrogen to form the unpleasant-smelling gas hydrogen sulfide, which has the aroma of rotten eggs. Treading on the surface of a bog sometimes causes this gas to be released in bubbles as it is squeezed out of the deeper peat. The hydrogen sulfide in the lower peat layers reacts with the silver wire to produce the black silver sulfide. In the upper layers, oxygen is present, so the silver wire does not become tarnished.

The conclusion from these two experiments is that the upper layer of peat, approximately eight inches in depth, is penetrated by air. The living mosses and roots and the dead remains of plants are not compacted here. There are ample spaces through which air can penetrate, and water likewise moves readily through this layer, rising in times of rain, and falling in times of drought. Wetland scientists call this aerated layer the *acrotelm,* and it is here that the bulk of decomposition takes place. The lower layers of peat, which scientists call the *catotelm,* are strongly compressed and compacted as a result of the weight of peat lying above them (see the illustration on page 82). As a consequence, there are no spaces between the dead plant remains, and neither air nor water can move easily. Oxygen is rapidly used up here, and decomposition virtually comes to a standstill. Decomposition never completely halts, however, because there are some bacteria that are able to continue digesting organic matter even in the absence of oxygen. But their activity is very slow, so once organic matter has become buried to the depth of the catotelm, it is fairly safe from the activities of the decomposers and may remain in a preserved and fossil state for many thousands, or even millions, of years.

The coal that people burn for energy is the remnant of very ancient catotelm peat, laid down many million years ago and now brought back into contact with oxygen as a result of human activity. Burning the coal oxidizes the organic remains that ancient microbes failed to decompose. It completes the energy flow process that has long been suspended, dissipating the energy that was trapped from the Sun by the wetland plants of long ago. It also completes a nutrient cycle that has long been on hold.

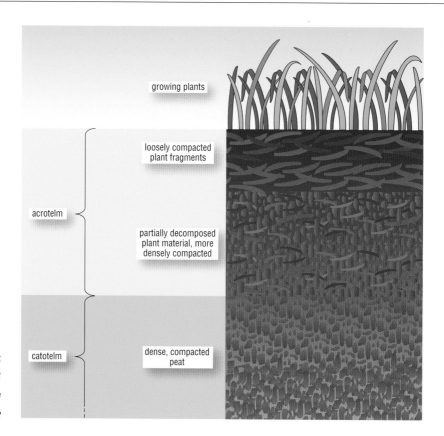

growing plants

loosely compacted plant fragments

acrotelm

partially decomposed plant material, more densely compacted

catotelm

dense, compacted peat

The upper layers (approximately 18 inches; 45 cm) of a peat profile

The entry and exit of nutrients

No ecosystem exists in total isolation from all others. Both energy and chemical elements are exchanged between ecosystems by biological movements (such as the wandering of animals) and by physical movements (such as the flow of water and air). Wetlands are no exception, and they both donate and receive energy and nutrients to and from other neighboring ecosystems. Understanding the paths by which elements enter and leave ecosystems is key to conserving them, and a knowledge of the quantities of elements moving along these paths is valuable if people wish to harvest materials from the ecosystem.

The atmosphere is common to all terrestrial ecosystems, and it provides a medium through which elements can move from one ecosystem to another. Carbon is one element that is obtained from the atmosphere by plants and used in the construction of their bodies. Carbon is a critical element for all living organisms because almost all energy storage and transfer involves compounds built using carbon atoms. The atmosphere carries carbon dioxide gas into a terrestrial ecosystem, and emergent plants in wetlands tap this resource for their photosynthesis. Carbon dioxide (CO_2) also enters the ecosystem in a dissolved form in rainfall and in the streams or rivers that flow into the wetland. This dissolved CO_2 is available for photosynthesis by submerged aquatic plants and phytoplankton. A third way in which carbon can enter a wetland is as the hydrogen carbonate ion, HCO_3^-. This may be derived from carbonic acid, formed by the reaction of carbon dioxide gas with water, or it may result from lime (calcium carbonate) dissolving in water. Once again, the hydrogen carbonate ion can be used by aquatic plants for their photosynthesis.

Much of the carbon fixed by photosynthesis in a wetland ecosystem is lost in respiration, but some becomes locked in the sediments that accumulate, especially in the peat deposits of the temperate bogs. There is currently much concern about the quantity of carbon that humans are injecting into the atmosphere as a result of burning fossil fuels (the carbon reserves of ancient wetlands). About 5.5 billion tons of carbon enters the atmosphere each year as a result of human combustion of these reserves, and more than half of this remains in the atmosphere, building up year after year and contributing to climate change. Of the remainder, some dissolves in the oceans and some is taken up by growing forests, but some is unaccounted for. There is a "missing sink" for carbon that has not yet been identified, and the uptake of carbon by peat lands is likely to be a part of this sink for atmospheric carbon. Peat deposits, as we have seen, grow only slowly, so the amount of carbon that can be taken up in a year is not great, but every small carbon sink is important in preventing the buildup of carbon dioxide in the atmosphere. The storage of carbon by wetlands is of global significance (see "Wetlands as carbon sinks," pages 160–162).

Nitrogen also enters wetland ecosystems from the atmosphere. The nitrogen gas that composes almost 80 percent of the atmosphere cannot be taken up directly by plants; it first has to be converted into ammonia and then to nitrates. Electrical storms can result in this reaction, but the total quantities fixed in this way are relatively small. Far more important is the capacity for some microbes to convert the relatively inert nitrogen gas into a form that can be used by plants. About 150 million tons of nitrogen is fixed each year by microbes globally. A further 150 million tons are fixed by industrial processes, particularly for use as fertilizers in agriculture. In wetlands there are several types of organisms that fix nitrogen. Blue-green bacteria (cyanobacteria) can carry out this process, and they are frequently found in many wetland ecosystems, especially in the Tropics. In Arctic wetlands some lichens fix nitrogen because they consist of a close association between a fungus and an alga or a blue-green bacterium. In the latter case it is the microbe that can fix nitrogen. Among higher plants, there are several that form associations (symbiosis) with nitrogen-fixing bacteria. The pea family (Fabaceae) is the best known of these, but relatively few plants in this family are important in wetlands. Alder trees have nodules in their roots in which bacteria reside and conduct their nitrogen-fixing activities, as do some other wetland plants, such as the bog myrtle (*Myrica gale*). All of these organisms are involved in the entry of nitrogen from the atmosphere to wetland ecosystems.

Nutrient elements also arrive in wetlands in rainfall. The chemistry of rainfall is strongly affected by the proximity of the ocean (see "Geology and water chemistry," pages 46–51). Far from the sea the rainfall tends to contain lower quantities of most elements. Industrial pollution also contributes to the chemistry of the rainfall, and this can have a significant effect on the nutrient cycling of wetlands. Among the most important of the aerial pollutants humans generate are nitrogen oxides and sulfur dioxide. Both of these are produced by fossil fuel burning, including the combustion of gasoline by automobiles. When rainfall washes these from the atmosphere, they arrive at the ground surface in the form of nitric acid and sulfuric acid—extremely corrosive compounds that attack buildings, human lungs, and plant tissues. Acid rain falls upon wetlands, particularly those in the northern regions that lie downwind of centers of industry, especially eastern Canada and Scandinavia. Aquatic ecosystems are particularly affected in spring when snowmelt results in a sudden surge of acidic water into wetlands, causing a rapid decline in the pH of the water (see the sidebar "Acidity and pH," pages 46–47). This damages sensitive species, including some phytoplankton and various animals. Ombrotrophic peat land ecosystems are less likely to be damaged by acidity in rainfall because their waters are already acid. In this type of ecosystem, where nutrient elements are in very short supply, the input of nitric acid results in a rise in nitrates, which act as a fertilizer to the nitrogen-starved vegetation. This can change the competitive balance of the vegetation and can result in some robust species taking over dominance and eliminating smaller specialist species, such as the carnivorous plants (see "Plants of the wetlands," pages 98–105).

Rainfall is the sole source of water for an ombrotrophic peat land, but the rheotrophic wetlands also receive water and a supply of dissolved elements from streams and rivers. Valley mires receive most of their nutrient supply in this way. The quantity of nutrients supplied in drainage water depends upon the nature of the rocks in the catchment (see "Geology and wetland landscapes," pages 42–46) and also upon the land use and ecosystem management in the surrounding areas. Some of the nitrogen fixed by industrial processes and spread on the ground as fertilizer by farmers finds its way into streams and rivers and from there drains into these wetlands, resulting in eutrophication. The speed of movement of water through the wetland also affects the

Cross section of a valley mire. A drainage stream runs through the valley and the additional flow of water along the stream brings a richer supply of nutrients, allowing a more luxurious development of vegetation, including trees. The lateral parts of the mire have a slower water flow and therefore poorer nutrient supplies. Consequently, poor fen or bog vegetation develops in these regions.

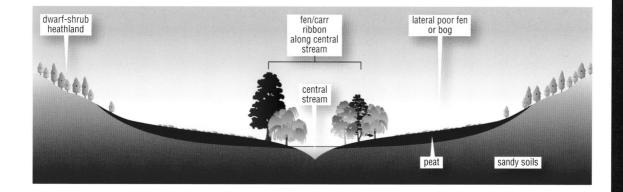

dwarf-shrub heathland

fen/carr ribbon along central stream

lateral poor fen or bog

central stream

peat

sandy soils

nutrient supply. Slow-moving water, as in the almost stag-nant sides of a valley mire, supply limited quantities of vital elements, whereas the fast-flowing stream at the center of a valley mire provide a relatively rich source of nutrients, even when their concentration in the water may be low (see illustration on page 85).

Animals may also bring nutrients into wetlands. Migrating geese, for example, spend some of their time grazing on the fertilized pastures that people intended for their domestic crops. Most grazing animals are able to detect and evidently prefer well-fertilized grassland, so they can pick out the best sources for nutrients such as nitrogen and phosphorus. They then make their way to wetlands, where they defecate and thus enrich the nutrient content of the ecosystem. In Africa the hippopotamus can act as a transfer system for nutrients. At night hippos leave the water and graze along the banks of rivers, sometimes invading and consuming the crops of local farmers. They return to the rivers in the daytime, and there they deposit their fecal material, rich in the fertilizing ele-ments that farmers have spread upon their lands. In the Pacific northwest of North America, salmon migrate from the oceans up into rivers in the spring, and here they breed and die. Their death and decomposition releases significant quan-tities of nutrients that have been collected from their ocean feeding, and these materials enrich the wetland ecosystems fed by the streams where they have bred and died.

Animals can also take nutrients out of a wetland ecosys-tem. The moose, for example, spends time in summer graz-ing on the aquatic plants of the wetlands that are scattered among the coniferous forests of the northern lands (see page 85). Scientists have sought to discover what it is about the aquatic plants that proves so attractive to moose, and the answer seems to be the element sodium. Sodium is not needed by plants, but animals need it for nerve function. In locations close to the ocean there is no shortage of sodium in the environment in the form of salt (sodium chloride), but away from the ocean sodium can become scarce. The aquatic plants of the boreal wetlands accumulate sodium, though no one as yet knows why. Whatever the reason, moose have evidently become aware of the sodium and

exploit these plants during their active growth period in the summer months. They harvest the sodium in their wetland grazing, and much is then transported into the forest, where some will be deposited in feces. Many wetland birds and mammals similarly harvest the produce of these ecosystems and transport the materials out of the wetland and into other surrounding ecosystems where they roost or breed. Ospreys, bald eagles, and grizzly bears all take fish from wetlands and transport some of the nutrient content to forest ecosystems.

One other major exit route for nutrients from wetland ecosystems is the stream or river that drains from the wetland. The water leaving a wetland may contain a higher or a lower concentration of elements than the water that originally entered the ecosystem. This depends upon the various other sources of nutrients and also upon the rate of growth of biomass and the rate of element storage in the sediments. In some wetlands erosion of sediments is important, and the water that leaves the ecosystem may contain suspended

The hippopotamus (Hippopotamus amphibius), *seen here with a cattle egret* (Bubulcus ibis) *perched upon its head, is a characteristic mammal of African wetlands. It is surrounded by an abundant floating aquatic weed of the Tropics,* Pistia stratiotes. *The hippo feeds upon riverside vegetation during the night, returning to the water during the day.* (Courtesy of Gerry Ellis/Minden Pictures)

organic or mineral matter. In order to compare the water-borne input and output, we need to know both the concentration of the elements in the water and the total volume of water flowing in and out of the system. This can be measured by constructing measuring stations upstream and downstream of the wetland and monitoring the flow and chemical constitution of the water.

If all the sources of entry and exit for nutrient elements in a wetland can be quantified, then a budget sheet can be constructed for each element. From this one can determine whether the ecosystem is gaining or losing any given element. This can be useful information, especially if people intend to exploit the wetland in some way. People may wish to harvest fish, or timber, or reeds for the construction of roofs, or cranberries for human consumption, or they may consider grazing domestic stock on a wetland. Knowledge of

Young moose feeding on aquatic vegetation at Camas National Wildlife Refuge, Camas, Idaho. Moose feed on aquatic plants during the summer because they are rich in elements such as sodium. (Courtesy of Carolyn McKendry)

the nutrient budget of the ecosystem helps in determining the possible harvest for any component of an ecosystem without incurring damage or running down its nutrient capital.

Nutrient cycling in wetlands

Once nutrient elements have entered a wetland, they may simply pass through with the flow of the water, but it is quite possible that they will be trapped by plants and then recycled within the system. Plants take up elements that they need mainly through their roots. Roots are constantly growing, and it is in the region just behind the growing tip that fine root hairs are formed. Root hairs are responsible for most of the water and mineral uptake. They are simple extensions of single cells, and their life span is very short, a few days at most, but in that time they capture the elements the plant will need for its growth. Between 5 and 10 percent of the roots of a plant die each day on average, so root replacement is vital and occurs constantly. In a wetland these roots are often immersed in water, usually embedded in the underlying sediment.

Roots are responsible for the absorption of the required elements from the water or the sediment, and this process means that the nutrients have to be taken from a low concentration and brought within the cell where their concentration is higher. Absorbing elements against a concentration gradient demands energy, and roots consume a great deal of a plant's energy. To provide this energy, roots need to respire. This means that they need oxygen, which is either supplied in solution in the surrounding water or is brought from the surface within the tissues of the plant. (Chapter 4 will examine the anatomical adaptations associated with this way of life.) Moving water replaces both the oxygen needed for respiration and the supply of nutrients taken up by the roots. Stagnant water becomes depleted in its content of both oxygen and mineral nutrients. In some wetlands it is possible to trace the course of water movement through the habitat by the richness of the vegetation that has developed. In valley mires, for example, as shown in the figure on page 85, water moves rapidly along a stream system that occupies the central part of the valley, and here the nutrient supply is maintained by the constant flow of water. As a consequence, the fast-flowing section of the wetland bears rich vegetation, often willow and alder trees. In the side areas of the valley the gradual seepage of water is much slower, and if the water is poor in nutrients, which is often the case on sandstone or granite bedrock, the slow-moving water fails to supply enough nutrients for rich vegetation to develop. These lateral parts of the wetland are relatively stagnant, acidic, and nutrient-poor and bear vegetation that often consists of bog mosses and other non-demanding species of plants.

When elements are taken up by a plant, they become incorporated into its structure, in cell walls, membranes, storage organs, flowers, and seeds. Animals feeding on the plants take not only the energy content of the material they consume but also the mineral elements that they need for their own body structure. Thus elements also pass through food webs. Not all plant material is eaten by herbivores; some survives until it becomes too worn for further use and then dies. But plants do not release their hard-won nutrients without a struggle. Dying leaves undergo a process in which their nutrient elements are mobilized and withdrawn from the leaf into the growing parts of the plant. When the dead leaf finally falls to the ground or into the water, it has been stripped of much of its nutrient content.

Dead plant and animal materials accumulate on the surface of the wetland sediments, which may be below the surface of the water or, in the case of peat lands, above the water surface. The same microbial decomposition that releases and dissipates the energy content of this litter also liberates the elements that remain in the decomposing organic matter. These elements may be taken up by plant roots and begin another cycle, or they may be taken out of the ecosystem in the flow of water. There is a third option: They may remain in the ecosystem as part of the accumulating body of sediments. If this happens, then they become locked into a growing reservoir of material that may remain undisturbed for thousands or even millions of years. Effectively, they are taken out of the nutrient cycle. The one event that can bring

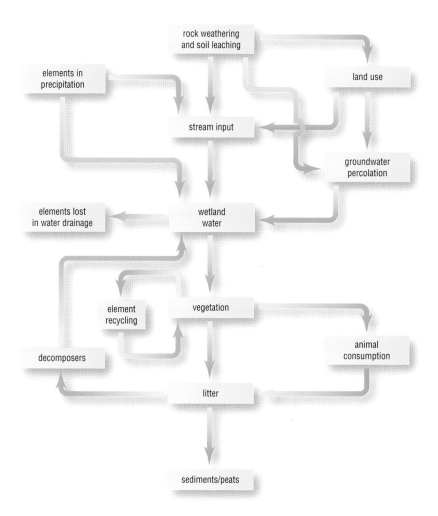

Nutrient cycling in a wetland ecosystem

them back into circulation is if a living root penetrates down to the depth where they are stored and absorbs them back into the living part of the ecosystem.

The diagram summarizes the nutrient cycle in a wetland together with the main import and export routes for nutrients in the inflowing and outflowing waters. As in the case of energy flow, the most unusual feature of the nutrient cycle of wetlands is that a store of nutrients is gradually built up in the form of the wetland sediments.

Conclusions

Ecosystems consist of both living and nonliving components, and they can be characterized by their patterns of energy flow and nutrient cycling. Wetlands are distinctive ecosystems in which the total amount of energy leaving the system is less than the total amount of energy entering the system. The residue of energy is stored as organic matter in the sediments or as peat. This residue accumulates as a result of incomplete decomposition, caused by the lack of oxygen for microbial activity in waterlogged, oxygen-scarce environments.

Decomposition occurs mainly in the surface layers of sediments and peat, where oxygen is most easily available. In a peat deposit the upper, loosely compacted layer where decomposition and water movement occur most rapidly is called the acrotelm. The more compacted deeper layer where decomposition and water movement is very slow is called the catotelm.

Nutrients enter wetland ecosystems through the atmosphere, in rainfall, in stream water, and by the movements of animals. The main loss is by exit streams and rivers. Like energy, which is used up (respired) more slowly than it is captured from solar radiation by photosynthesis, nutrients accumulate in wetland ecosystems as a result of the buildup of sediments in which nutrients become locked away and stored indefinitely.

CHAPTER 4

WETLAND BIODIVERSITY

Biodiversity encompasses the range of living things, the degree of genetic variation, and the wealth of different habitats found within any particular ecosystem. Wetlands vary greatly in their biodiversity, some being relatively poor and others extremely rich. But even those that have few species should not be considered poor in value because the species that exist there are often found in no other habitat on Earth. All wetlands, therefore, contribute to global biodiversity.

The wetland habitat is distinct from any land-based, terrestrial habitat. Its wetness means that the plant and animal species found within it are often confined to this type of ecosystem. Wetland organisms face specific environmental problems, and different types of animals and plants have overcome these problems, either by developing a particular structural adaptation or by their distinctive behavior. Wetlands are also found in many different types of climates in various parts of the world, so they are not confined to certain areas or particular zones of latitude as are most of the great global biomes, such as rain forest, savanna, and desert. Because they may occur almost anywhere on Earth, wetlands have evolved their own collection of animals and plants within each of the major climatic belts, and this means that, taken as a whole, wetlands are a great source of global biodiversity.

Living in the wet

It may seem an obvious fact, but wetlands usually have an abundance of water, and it is this aspect of their ecology that determines the way in which wetland plants and animals live. On the whole, therefore, in contrast to the desert environment, the organisms of wetlands do not encounter difficulty in obtaining the water they need for life. Although there are some wetlands that periodically become dry, and these present some very distinct problems to their inhabitants, as will be seen, the main problem in wetlands is that water is so abundant that it creates other challenges. Travel from one place to another, for example, requires flight or swimming on the part of animals, and air or water dispersal for the seeds of plants. Various lifestyles are available in the wetland. Plants and animals may spend their entire lives either above water or below water, or they may spend some time in each. Some animals and microbes spend their whole lives in the permanent dark wetness of the sediments, either in basal mud or in the accumulating layers of organic peat. Others, like the birds of reed beds, may spend their lives entirely above the water, living among the stems of reeds and never getting their feet wet. The problems of living in the wet are therefore quite varied, depending on which strategy is adopted.

Beneath the water surface, and particularly in the water-logged sediments of a wetland, one of the main problems is lack of oxygen. Even the microbes in the mud and peat of wetlands find it difficult to obtain enough oxygen to complete the process of organic decomposition (see "Decomposition," pages 79–82). The very slow diffusion of dissolved oxygen means that once it has been taken out of the water by microbes, mud-dwelling animals, and the roots of plants, it is replaced only very slowly. As a result, only those creatures that can cope with very low levels of oxygen can survive in such a stressed environment.

Some microbes resort to using alternatives to oxygen. For example, the sulfate ion (SO_4^{2-}) contains some oxygen and can be used in respiration as an alternative. The result is the production of the sulfide ion (S^{2-}), which then combines with iron to produce the black compound iron sulfide (FeS) or with hydrogen to make hydrogen sulfide (H_2S), an evil-smelling gas that bubbles from the black sediments of stagnant waters. There are very few animals that can live in these conditions. There are two main ways by which an organism can overcome this degree of oxygen starvation. One is to develop biochemical pathways that avoid the need for oxygen, and the other is to transport oxygen from above the water to the anoxic (oxygen deficient) environment in the sediments.

Normal, aerobic respiration (that is, respiration in the presence of oxygen) leads to the conversion of an organic compound, such as sugar into carbon dioxide and water, but this process needs oxygen to form the carbon dioxide. If oxygen is not present, the respiratory process can stop short of carbon dioxide production and lead to the buildup of ethanol. This is the reaction that is exploited in the production of alcohol; beer and wine are fermented using the anaerobic respiration of the microbe yeast. This process does result in some energy production for the organism, but less than the full oxidation of organic matter to carbon dioxide would produce. The problem with the technique is that ethanol is toxic to cells, so any accumulation of the compound can inhibit cell function. This is why beer and wines have a maximum alcohol content of about 15 percent; above that level the yeast cells are killed. Plant roots under anoxic conditions also resort to anaerobic respiration, just like a yeast, but ethanol accumulation proves harmful. Some plant species, however, particularly the plants of permanently waterlogged wetlands, have developed a way around the problem. They divert the biochemical pathway from the production of toxic ethanol to that of malic acid, a relatively harmless compound. This is an example of how a wetland species can modify its biochemistry to overcome the difficulties it experiences when rooted in anoxic mud.

Some wetland animals that live in submerged and oxygen-deficient habitats have developed compounds that bond with oxygen and help to circulate it in their bodies. The red pigment hemoglobin, which gives blood its distinctive color, is also present in some wetland invertebrate animals, including some worms, mollusks, and midges, and assists them in storing and moving oxygen. The African catfish (*Bagrus* species) has a form of hemoglobin with a very strong affinity for oxygen, which enables it to cope with low oxygen and high carbon dioxide concentrations.

The alternative technique is to carry oxygen from a place where it is abundant, such as the air above the water surface.

Emergent plants can do this by constructing passages in their stems along which oxygen can diffuse from the atmosphere to the submerged roots. Mobile animals can swim to the surface, gather air bubbles over their bodies, and carry them down into tunnels in the mud or into nest structures so that they have their own supply of air in a hostile, airless environment.

The water layers above the sediments are usually less oxygen deficient than mud is because they are in motion; oxygen is constantly dissolving at the surface and diffusing slowly downward. Also, green algae and pondweeds may be photosynthesizing and producing oxygen as a waste product that they liberate into the water. Animals living in this zone, however, have to be able to obtain their oxygen from the water, which means that they need gills. Gills are organs that are found in fish, in the larvae of amphibians, and in many aquatic invertebrates, and they work by passing water over a surface rich in blood contained within thin-walled vessels. Oxygen from the water is able to diffuse through cell walls and enter the bloodstream. In order to achieve this, gills have a very large surface area and may be situated internally (as in fish) or externally (as in many invertebrates). Internal gills operate by having a constant flow of water over their surfaces, usually achieved by the motion of the fish through the water or by the pumping action of the gill covers.

Living above the surface of the water demands very different adaptations. For a plant, one of the main problems is support, because air does not provide the buoyancy of water. Leaves of water lilies float because of the air sacs in their tissues and the density of water lying beneath them. They have no need of woody structures to hold them erect. The stems of rushes, on the other hand, need specially strengthened ridges to hold the green photosynthetic stems vertically above the water. On the positive side, however, air circulates freely around the stems and leaves of emergent plants, so they can open their stomatal pores and take in carbon dioxide without difficulty. This gas is not abundant in the atmosphere (only about 0.035 percent by volume) but it diffuses rapidly in air, so it is quickly replenished when absorbed by plants. The slow diffusion of dissolved carbon dioxide in water means that submerged aquatic plants on a bright

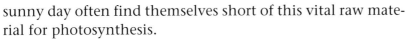

sunny day often find themselves short of this vital raw material for photosynthesis.

Animals above the water also have the advantage of free gaseous exchange, so that the supply of oxygen is not a problem. The gill, however, is no longer an appropriate organ for taking in oxygen because it would rapidly become dry and gaseous oxygen could not dissolve in the surface water. The alternative for vertebrate animals is the lung, which functions very much like a gill but is enclosed within the body to minimize water loss from its surface. Air has to be pumped in and out of the lung so that the supply of oxygen is maintained and the waste carbon dioxide can be expelled. In insects there are no distinct lungs, but tubes called *tracheae* extend throughout the body and carry air to all parts. These tubes open by *spiracles* on the outside of the insects' casing, and oxygen diffuses through the tracheae and is absorbed across their linings into the blood. Although this diffusion is adequate for the supply of oxygen to most small insects, larger ones and those that are very active need a faster air movement, and they achieve this by pumping air in and out of the tracheae by expanding and contracting their body walls.

As discussed previously, the chemistry of water has a strong influence on the plant and animal life of wetlands (see "Geology and water chemistry," pages 46–51). Acidity, in particular, determines whether certain organisms are able to survive at a site. Some elements, such as iron and aluminum, are more soluble in acid water than in alkaline conditions, and their availability in acid wetlands can result in toxic reactions in some species. Acidification of a wetland can lead to the loss of many species because of increased aluminum toxicity. Many plant species have a specific demand for calcium, and this element, as calcium carbonate, is associated with high pH conditions. Any animal that builds a lime shell, such as some bivalve and gastropod mollusks, also needs alkaline, calcium-rich conditions. Generally speaking, wetlands with a pH above 7 are richer in plant and animal species than acid sites.

The other chemical factor that strongly affects biodiversity in wetlands is salinity. Coastal wetlands naturally tend to be saline because of the sea's influence. Seawater has about 3 percent of salt content, so a wetland that is regularly flooded by the sea, such as the mouths of estuaries, will have an elevated level of salt. The presence of dissolved salts in water presents problems of water balance for freshwater plants and animals. If an organism that lives and grows in freshwater is placed in seawater, it soon dies because it fails to take up water from its surroundings. An organism from a saline habitat placed in freshwater, on the other hand, is likely to absorb water too rapidly and cause the rupture of its membranes. Different species of animals and plants are therefore found occupying wetlands that have different salinities. In estuaries one may even find a series of different species occupying certain ranges within the spectrum of salinities found with increasing distance from the ocean.

Other problems that wetland organisms may encounter include drought and fire. Some wetlands undergo regular dry periods, often on a seasonal basis, being filled with water in a winter or wet season and dried out in a summer or dry season. Fluctuation of water levels means that organisms need to be able to cope with either wet or dry conditions, and this is very demanding. Relatively few species thrive under the two extremes, so emigration or survival through the unfavorable period (usually the dry season) is the best strategy. Fire in wetlands is unlikely to affect the underwater life directly, but it can lead to an input of charcoal and mineral matter eroded from surrounding catchment areas. Organisms living above the water surface, on the other hand, such as the closely packed beds of tall reeds, can be very fire prone, especially in winter when the reeds are dry. (People have sometimes used fire to manage this type of habitat because it assists in removing excess dead biomass; see "Wetland rehabilitation and conservation," pages 179–182.)

These are the main problems facing organisms that seek to survive in the wetlands. The major groups of plants and animals found in wetland habitats have developed a variety of mechanisms for coping with these difficulties.

Plants of the wetlands

There are three options for a plant growing in a wetland. It can grow underwater, rooted in the mud; it can float submerged in the water without any attachment to the sediments; or it can spread its shoots and leaves above the water while keeping its roots beneath the surface. Submerged, bottom-rooted plants can survive only while light penetration is adequate, so there is a limit to how deep they can grow. Light penetration in water depends on *turbidity,* that is, the degree of disturbance to the water by wave action and currents, and also on the quantity of suspended sediment in the water. At a depth of 50 feet (15 m), even in clear, calm water, the light intensity may be only 10 percent of that at the surface. So plants that root at the bottom usually occupy the shallow water.

It is possible for a plant to root in the mud and then have very long stems or leaf stalks so that the photosynthetic tissues can be closer to the surface. In the case of the water lily (*Nymphaea* species), the stems are buried in the mud, but each floating leaf is connected to the stem by a long, thin leaf stalk. The stalk is hollow to carry air down to the submerged and buried stem, but there is a limit to how long a leaf stalk can grow. For the water lily the growth limit is about 13 feet (4 m), and this restricts the depth of water that water lilies can occupy. Like the submerged aquatic plants, they are therefore found mainly in shallow water or around the margins of deeper pools. These two growth strategies influence each other because a dense growth of water lily leaves on the surface greatly reduces the light penetration to the bottom, shading out species that are entirely submerged.

Among the most familiar of free-floating aquatic plants is the duckweed (family Lemnaceae). There are several species, but typically the duckweed consists of a small floating green disc with one or more roots extending from its underside. The disc is actually a stem rather than a leaf as it might appear, because the root arises directly from it, as does the flower. Reproduction, however, is chiefly by vegetative means, each disc budding off new individuals. Under good conditions, vegetative division occurs rapidly and a whole pond can become covered in duckweed over a matter of days. There are some species of duckweed, such as the ivy-leaved duckweed, that float not on the surface but a little way below it. These submerged plants suffer the disadvantage that they might be shaded by the development of the floating carpet of discs on the surface, but they are specially adapted to life in the partial shade and can survive within the lower light levels.

One floating aquatic that has become a serious weed in many of the wetlands of the world is the water hyacinth (*Eichhornia crassipes*). This forms floating bunches of leaves with very attractive blue-purple flowers. A native of the wetlands of Brazil in South America, it has been spread around the tropical world by humans, who found its flowers appealing but failed to appreciate the consequences of accidental introduction. Rapid vegetative reproduction has led to the total cover of many areas of formerly open water and the blockage of commercial waterways.

Emergent aquatics, including cattails (*Typha* species), reeds (*Phragmites australis*), and bulrushes (*Schoenoplectus* species) succeed in the competition for light by extending their stems above the surface of the water. By occupying the air above the water surface in this way, emergent plants provide a new spatial dimension for living creatures. The ecosystem has a more complex architecture with its new aerial environment, so animals including insects, mollusks, and birds have a new set of opportunities for living, feeding, and breeding. As with the leaf stalks of water lilies, most of the stems of reeds and rushes are hollow and carry air to their roots through the channels in their tissues. These tubes also carry waste gases from the roots back to the air, especially carbon dioxide, derived from root respiration. If the stem of a reed is damaged or cut, it leaks the gas methane from the submerged mud into the atmosphere. This is of no functional significance to the plant, but it is an important aspect of the global cycling of carbon and is a significant source of this greenhouse gas in the atmosphere.

Tree growth in wetland swamps results in even greater competition for light and even more complex structure in the architecture of the habitat. Birds may roost or nest in the canopy, and small plants may find sites they can occupy on the branches of the trees, spending their entire lives without touching the soil beneath. These plants are called *epiphytes,* and they include the Spanish moss that clothes the superstructures of trees in the southeastern United States. Spanish moss (*Tillandsia* species) is a member of the Bromeliad family, which has many members in the tropical forested swamps of the world. Along with the orchids, it is one of the most widespread of epiphytic plant families.

The bald or swamp cypress (*Taxodium distichum*) is one of the most famous and typical of swamp trees, living with its roots submerged and its tapering, conical trunk rising up out of the waters. Like all plants rooted in water, it needs to provide oxygen for its roots, and it achieves this in part by having rounded structures called "knees" on its roots that stand above the water table and permit gaseous exchange. The wood of aquatic trees also needs to be particularly resistant to attack by fungi, and this is true of both bald cypress and the alder (*Alnus* species), another tree of the swamps. Because the woods of these trees are naturally resistant to decay, they have often been used for jetty construction and in other situations where the wood is constantly exposed to water.

There are some ferns that grow in wetlands, among them the tropical floating ferns *Pistia* and *Salvinia,* which, like the water hyacinth, have attained pest proportions in some wetlands (see the photograph on page 87), including those of Australia, where they have been introduced. In the marshes and swamps of the temperate zone, however, there are relatively few ferns that achieve any great importance. The marsh fern (*Thelypteris palustris*) and the royal fern (*Osmunda regalis*) are perhaps the most abundant, though these species have become scarce in Europe because of the Victorian craze for collecting ferns and growing them in gardens, as a result of which some wetland habitats were stripped of their ferns.

Mosses, on the other hand, play a very important part in wetland ecology, particularly the group of bog mosses called *sphagnum.* The bog mosses have an unusual structure (see the illustrations on page 102). They have upright stems with dense heads, or *capitula,* and they grow in dense hummocks creating miniature sponges. Their cell structure is also distinctive, the leaves containing thin green cells with chlorophyll surrounding large dead cells that become filled with water. The stems also have empty cells with a flasklike structure that can become water-filled. The result is that a bunch of sphagnum can hold a very large quantity of water. A

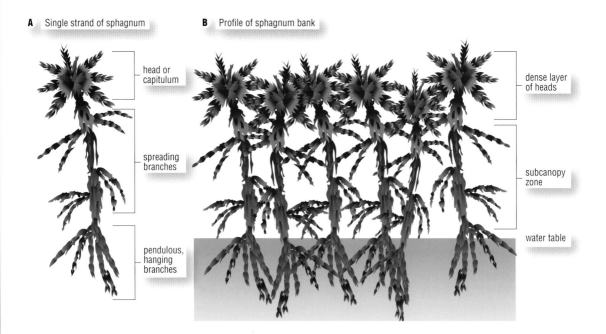

A Single strand of sphagnum

head or capitulum

spreading branches

pendulous, hanging branches

B Profile of sphagnum bank

dense layer of heads

subcanopy zone

water table

The structure of the bog moss, sphagnum. A. Single strand of sphagnum, showing the dense head and the clusters of branches. B. A carpet of sphagnum has a distinct architecture, with a flat layer of heads on the top and a shaded, moist zone beneath the canopy.

sample of sphagnum moss weighed when saturated and then again after drying will have lost about 95 percent of its weight. When this plant begins to grow in a wetland, it creates an entirely new environment in which saturated plant matter builds up in mounds among the other vegetation.

Bog mosses also have peculiar chemical properties. Their cell walls are able to attract and hold elements from the water. They take up the cations (positively charged atoms) from the surrounding water and replace them with hydrogen ions (protons), which are also positively charged. In this way the plant wall behaves like an acid, and the pH of the surrounding water falls (see the sidebar "Acidity and pH," pages 46–47). Thus the growth of sphagnum in a wetland results in an increase of water holding, an increase in acidity, and a decrease in the fertility of the water. The outcome is the death of many other plants. Even trees eventually die; if not killed directly, they are prevented from producing offspring when their seeds fail to germinate and establish, sealing their fate. Bog mosses may not look very sinister, but their arrival at a wetland, transported through the air in the form of tiny spores, spells big changes to the vegetation composition and the beginnings of bog development.

In the acid bogs that sphagnum produces there are some plants that still survive and thrive. Many of these belong to the blueberry family (Ericaceae) including bog rosemary (*Andromeda polifolia*), leatherleaf (*Chamaedaphne calyculata*), and Labrador tea (*Ledum groenlandicum*). All of these have evergreen leaves, which may seem surprising as this type of leaf is usually associated with coniferous forests or with chaparral vegetation (scrub found in Mediterranean climates, such as California). The leaves are also tough and leathery, which is what one might expect in a dry habitat rather than a wet one. Ecologists have long debated what advantages there might be in a bog plant having tough evergreen leaves. Some think that despite the abundance of water in the habitat the plants fail to absorb it, either because their roots are

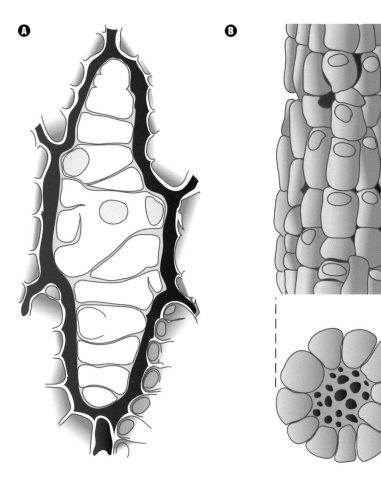

Cell structure of the bog moss, sphagnum.
A. Leaf cells. Narrow chlorophyll-containing cells surround a dead colorless cell with pores that permit them to become filled with water. Bands of wall thickening act as supports to these large dead cells. B. Stem. A stem of sphagnum has outer layers of large cells, some of which have pores and act as water-retaining vessels.

too cold or because of some toxin, such as iron or aluminum, in the acid soil. An alternative explanation is that many of the elements needed for constructing leaves, such as nitrogen, phosphorus, potassium, and magnesium, are in very short supply on a bog, because the only source is the rainwater. An evergreen leaf can last for up to three years, whereas a deciduous one lasts for only one season, so the bog plant gets more out of its nutrient investment when it produces evergreen leaves.

The shortage of nutrients on the bog surface also accounts for a very unusual type of organism, the carnivorous plant. Animal tissues are much richer in nitrogen than plant tissues because they contain a larger proportion of protein. When a plant is short of nitrogen, therefore, what could be more beneficial than to feed upon animals? The problem is that animals are mobile while plants are not, so trapping requires some ingenuity. Carnivorous plants come in a number of different forms, employing different methods of catching their prey. The simplest is the sticky trap, as found in the sundews (*Drosera* species) and the butterworts (*Pinguicula* species). Both of these have leaves covered in two types of glands: One is sticky and is responsible for entangling a visiting insect, while the other type secretes digestive enzymes and absorbs the products of the dissolving animal even before it is dead. A second method is the use of a spring trap, as in the case of the Venus flytrap (*Dionaea muscipula*) and the bladderwort (*Utricularia* species). Sensitive hairs alert the plant to the presence of a visitor and, in the case of the flytrap, this leads to the rapid loss of water from hinge cells in the leaf, and the trap snaps shut with the insect inside. The speed of movement is remarkable for a plant; it has to be fast enough to enclose a fly before it can take to the wing. Not only insects are trapped in this way. Even small amphibians can end up enclosed and subjected to slow digestion.

The third main trapping system that carnivorous plants employ is the pitfall trap, as used by pitcher plants (including the genera *Sarracenia* and *Darlingtonia*). These plants have curved, hornlike leaves, partially filled with water and digestive enzymes. The upper lip of the horn is brightly colored to attract insects but is coated by loose scales of slippery wax.

Even a fly with its prodigious ability to grip a surface with its hairy feet will lose its balance on this surface and end up falling into the digestive cauldron below. In all of these cases the prime objective is not the energy contained within the prey, which is what animal predators are most concerned to obtain, but certain chemical elements, particularly nitrogen. All of these carnivorous plants are photosynthetic, so obtaining energy is no problem to them; but in a world that is elevated above the influence of drainage water and where rain is the only source of nutrient elements, extreme measures are called for if plants are to obtain this scarce resource.

Microscopic life

Wetlands are rich in minute creatures that occupy their waters and their sediments. In the open water of the wetland habitat reside the plankton, microscopic plants, and animals that spend their short lives in the surface waters. The plankton can be divided into the *phytoplankton,* which are photosynthetic and therefore contribute to the primary production of the wetland, and the *zooplankton,* which are consumer organisms, feeding upon the phytoplankton and upon one another.

Most of the phytoplankton consists of one-celled organisms, such as the desmids (family Desmidaceae), green algae that can become so abundant as to give their green color to the water. The diatoms (protists belonging to the phylum Baccillariophyta) are another important group, which are unusual in having their one-celled bodies encased in a stiff box made of silica. Usually diatoms live singly, but some species form colonies, as in the case of *Asterionella,* the sticklike cells of which gather together in radial colonies that look like stars. The tiny cells of these organisms are so small that they are suspended in the water and remain near the surface. The diatoms are even able to move around by producing a stream of protoplasm along a groove in their side and propelling themselves through the water.

Other microscopic algae form long chains, or *filaments* and these can cover the whole surface of a wetland with a green blanket. One of the most common is *Cladophora,* sometimes

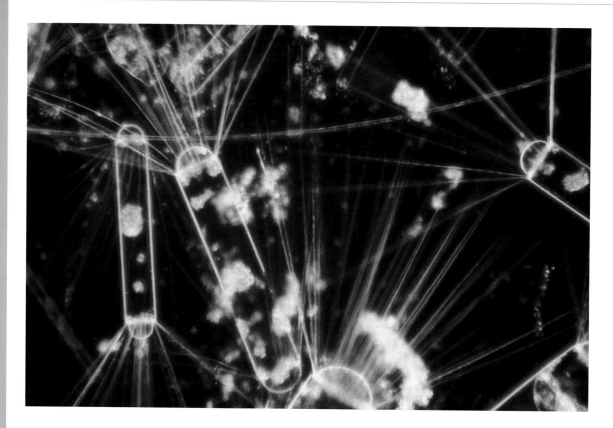

Diatoms. These are microscopic members of the photosynthetic plankton in wetlands. They consist of ornate cases called frustules that are made of silica. (Courtesy of Frans Lanting/ Minden Pictures)

referred to as "blanket weed" because of its ability to envelop a whole pool. Its filaments are branched and feel coarse to the touch. The reason for its coarse feel is that it produces no slimy mucilage on its surface, unlike the related *Spirogyra,* which has a very smooth feel and is so slippery it is difficult to pick up. The lack of mucilage around the filaments of *Cladophora* allows many other microscopic plants and animals to become attached to it. Beneath the microscope its surface looks like a miniature forest of diatoms and sedentary protists, such as *Vorticella,* a stalked microscopic creature that filters the water to catch and consume bacteria. Among the filamentous organisms are the blue-green bacteria, or cyanobacteria, which were once regarded as algae but are no longer regarded as plants, even though they photosynthesize. These are very abundant in tropical wetlands, including such cultivated wetlands as rice paddies. Not only do they fix carbon dioxide in photosynthesis, they also fix nitrogen and thus add to the fertility of a wetland.

Biologists no longer include algae and the unicellular phytoplankton as true plants but group them together in their own kingdom, the Protoctista, which they share with some organisms that were once regarded as animals and fungi. There are many consumer organisms among these protists, some of which have whiplike appendages, called *flagella,* which enable them to swim around and to engulf their prey. Others are covered with tiny hairs, or cilia, that flow in a wavelike motion and enable them to move around in search of food. Then there are the amoebas (genus *Amoeba* in the phylum Rhizopoda), cells of jellylike protoplasm that move by pushing out flexible masses of tissue and flow over the surface of the sediment. One particular group of amoebas is unusual in possessing a shell. These are called rhizopods (also in the phylum Rhizopoda). They are found in abundance in the upper layers of peat, and here the shell is of great importance because the water level is constantly changing, depending on how recently it has rained. So there is always a possibility of becoming dry for a short while, and the rhizopod can withdraw its delicate protoplasm into the shell. When the rhizopod dies, the shell is left intact and is preserved within the peat, leaving a record of the past existence of these tiny protists.

One remarkable unicellular protist is euglena (genus *Euglena* in the phylum Discomitochondria). It contains the green pigment chlorophyll and can photosynthesize, so it looks like an alga. It has a whiplike extension with which it can swim and a cell wall that is flexible so that it can wriggle like a worm. But the most unusual feature is that when it is kept in the dark and cannot rely on photosynthesis as a source of energy, it consumes organic detritus just like an amoeba. The chlorophyll disappears, and the organism turns white instead of green. When light is available again, the euglena becomes photosynthetic once more. Within the ecosystem, therefore, it can act either as a producer or a consumer. In wetlands it is quite common, especially in eutrophic conditions in small, stagnant ponds.

Other microscopic animals act entirely as consumers, however, such as the ciliate paramecium (genus *Paramecium* in the phylum Ciliphora). This one-celled protist is covered with fine short hairs, or cilia, which are in a constant state of motion enabling the organism to swim in a spiral fashion through the water and also to direct the water flow into a kind of gullet, where food material, particularly bacteria, is filtered out and consumed.

There are many swimming microscopic creatures in the waters of wetlands, some of which seek larger prey than bacteria. These organisms, which include rotifers and small crustaceans such as the water flea daphnia, are true animals. They are multicellular creatures with far more complex structures than the protists. The rotifers (phylum Rotifera), for example, are equipped with a mouth and stomach. Like paramecium, they swim with the aid of cilia and filter water for their food, but they extract larger fragments of organic detritus than the protists can manage. They have a foot by which they can attach themselves temporarily to a plant stem or an algal filament, and they can continue feeding while static. The small crustaceans are even more complicated in their structure and behavior. They have two pairs of sensory antennae and are also equipped with eyes, so they can hunt and forage more effectively than the rotifers. Among the microscopic wetland species are *Daphnia* and *Cyclops,* which resemble minute shrimps (also crustaceans, that is, belonging to the phylum Crustacea), and are both important and common members of the zooplankton.

The freshwaters of wetlands, whether the shallows of a marsh, the drainage channels of a swamp, or the pools of a bog, all contain a world of microscopic life. In many respects they can be regarded as small ecosystems in their own right, carrying out their functions of energy flow, food interchange, nutrient cycling, and decomposition within the greater ecosystem of the wetland. But they interact with their larger-scale surroundings, providing a food resource that supplies many other parts of the wetland ecosystem.

Invertebrates of the wetland

Invertebrate animals are found in abundance both above and below the surface of the water. Some spend their entire life underwater, while others begin their life in an aquatic medium and end it in the air. An aquatic life in a wetland presents many opportunities for different methods of feeding, leading to complicated food web development (see "Food webs and energy flow," pages 74–79). Some invertebrates prey upon the microscopic animals and plants in the plankton by catching and swallowing them, while others have a more static existence and filter their food out of the water. Some invertebrates are scrapers, rasping the surfaces of stones for the microscopic algae that coat them. Some live a lowly life, feeding on detritus down in the mud at the bottom of the wetland.

Among the active invertebrate hunters, the larvae of dragonflies (suborder Anisoptera) rank as the most fearsome. The larva's head consists of a hinged mask, which can be extended rapidly to seize its prey. Some are quite large and are able to tackle tadpoles or even small fish. This predator often lurks in a hiding place and then rushes out when its prey is least suspecting an attack. The larvae of caddis flies (order Trichoptera) are smaller and also slower because they are hampered by having to carry a tubular home that encloses their abdomens. They build these tubes out of sand grains or pieces of vegetable matter that they stick together with mucus. Some bugs, called pond skaters (family Geridae), occupy the surface of the water. Their long legs do not penetrate the surface tension of the water, so they can skate around rapidly and grab their prey with their forelegs.

Filter feeders include many of the bivalve mollusks (phylum Mollusca, class Bivalvia), which sit in the mud at the bottom of the wetland and suck in water with its content of microscopic life. They have tiny mobile hairs, or cilia, over their gills, and by moving these they can generate a flow of water, from which they extract their food. Food is conveyed to the bivalve's mouth in a constant stream of mucus. The material these animals consume includes both living and dead matter. Bacteria form part of their food, which is why mollusks sometimes contain toxins that cause food poisoning in humans.

The scraper feeders also include mollusks, but these are the snails (class Gastropoda), which have rasping tongues fitted with hard projections for peeling off the layers of organic material covering stones. Also falling into this feeding group are the flatworms (phylum Platyhelminthes), which flow like tiny slugs over the plant and mineral surfaces, scraping off their food. These small organisms are remarkable for their powers of regeneration. If they are cut in half, then each half is capable of growing back into a complete organism.

The detritus feeders live in the mud, and this group includes many types of worms, both the segmented types (phylum Annelida) and the unsegmented nematodes (phylum Nematoda), which are particularly abundant. They feed by consuming all that lies before them, passing the mud through their guts and extracting those materials that provide them with energy. Detritus feeders, including worms and mites, are also abundant in peat sediments, being found mainly in the upper, aerated layers of the acrotelm.

Among the wetland invertebrates that live below water in their early life and in the air when they are mature, the most familiar is the mosquito (family Culicidae). The mature insect feeds upon sugars from flowers for much of the time, but prior to breeding the female takes a meal of blood, and this is when people are most likely to encounter this unwelcome insect. In fact, mosquitoes will feed on the blood of almost any vertebrate, with the exception of fish. There is even one fish, the mudskipper of coastal mangrove wetlands, which does suffer from mosquito attacks because it spends much of its time on mud surfaces above water level. Although the bite of the mosquito can be irritating, it does not normally cause serious problems unless the insect was infected with viruses or other parasites, such as the malaria parasite (see "Wetlands and disease," pages 135–139).

Life above water is full of opportunities for insects, especially the plant feeders. Emergent plants are consumed by many insect larvae, including the caterpillars of moths and butterflies (order Lepidoptera). The common reed is often infested with a moth caterpillar that pupates (turns into a chrysalis) within its hollow stem. Mature moths and butterflies, along with bees, wasps, and flies often avail themselves of the nectar and pollen produced by wetland flowers. Fens are among the richest of wetland habitats for flowers, and insects abound in these ecosystems during the summer.

Mature dragonflies continue their predatory lives into their adulthood and patrol the marshes and fens for their insect prey. Mayflies (order Ephemeroptera), which often occur in dense swarms above the water surface, have spent their larval existence as detritus feeders beneath the water, but when they emerge above the surface in their maturity they do not feed at all. They have very tiny and useless mouthparts, so their lives are necessarily short, and their only function is to mate and die. Mayflies may spend as long as two years in their submerged larval state, only to emerge one morning and die by the evening.

Fish, amphibians, and reptiles

The open pools and channels of wetlands support a host of fish species that find a number of different ways to make a living. Bottom-living fish scavenge for detritus and for the insects that live and breed in the basal mud. Among these fish, bullheads and catfish (family Ictaluridae) are preeminent, especially in the southern and eastern United States. Both of these have barbels, or whiskers on their mouths, which they use as sensory organs to locate their food; they also have a keen sense of smell. Bullheads are mostly found in slow-moving waters and pools with an abundance of emergent vegetation, while the catfish prefer larger creeks with a stronger movement of water.

Eels also spend much time in the muddy deposits of wetlands, but they then migrate to the ocean, particularly the Gulf of Mexico and the Caribbean, where they breed. American eels (*Anguilla rostrata*) share their breeding grounds with the European eel (*Anguilla anguilla*), which must travel more than 3,000 miles to reach them, but the American and European eels do not seem to be confused when breeding, and the two species remain distinct from each other. Perhaps they use different areas within the oceans or different times for their breeding activity. Much remains to be discovered about these remarkable fish.

Predatory fish of the wetlands include grass pickerel (*Esox americanus*), muskie (*Esox masquinongy*), and largemouth bass (*Micropterus salmoides*). These are voracious feeders that hide in the shelter of overhanging and floating marsh vegetation and seize passing fish and amphibians as their prey. As is the case for most top predators, they are large in size but tend to be few in numbers compared with those lower in the food web. Their size and their strength, however, have made them popular as sport fish. In addition, they are very palatable to humans, so are heavily hunted. The popularity of large predatory fish taken for sport or human food has led to some unfortunate developments in wetland fisheries. In East Africa the powerful Nile perch (*Lates niloticus*) was introduced into Lake Victoria as a means of increasing the diversity of fish present, but the effect was precisely the opposite. The new and efficient predator quickly decreased the population of the native cichlid fishes and has brought some species close to extinction. Local fisheries were deprived of many of their usual species as the Nile perch assumed dominance in the wetlands fringing the lake.

The boundary between a marsh and the open water is an extremely important habitat for fish, especially when they are breeding. Some fish called tilapia (genus *Tilapia*) in Lake Victoria, for example, dig holes among the roots of emergent plants and lay their eggs with them. They then guard the eggs against predators and continue to brood and protect the young hatchlings. The stickleback (family Gasterosteidae) goes a step further and constructs a nest out of strands of vegetation that is shaped like a bottle with a neck and opening at one end. The male entices the female into the nest where she lays her eggs and he fertilizes them. Then he guards the eggs and even fans the nest opening with his tail to ensure a good movement of water and a rich supply of oxygen.

The Amazon basin is home to around 3,000 species of fish, and these take advantage of the floods that occur each spring when the snow melts on the Andes Mountains and water floods down into the forested plains. Rivers overflow their banks and trees that once occupied dry land stand in deep water. Fish from the rivers then find that their habitat is greatly expanded, and they swim among the tree trunks, foraging for new sources of food. One such source is provided by the seed and fruit production of the trees. Fish of many species collect these, and some seeds pass through their guts and are actually dispersed by fish. Piranha fish (family Characidae) have a reputation for flesh eating, but there are some species of piranha that are entirely vegetarian and join the seed hunters in the flooded forest. The floods also take fish into higher layers of the canopy than they have previously encountered, and they hunt insects on the leaves by leaping clear of the water to catch them, or even squirting water from their mouths to knock their prey from their perches. Not even the hummingbirds are safe from the voracious leaping fish that have invaded their habitat.

Amphibians are particularly important members of the wetland fauna, for they can take advantage of both the aquatic and the terrestrial conditions. Most amphibians require the water for their breeding because they lay eggs encased in jelly, either in large masses or in long chains, and these eggs would quickly desiccate if they were not immersed in water. Of all the North American amphibians, the bullfrog (*Rana catesbeiana*) is probably the most familiar. Its deep, penetrating voice is a frequent sound throughout the eastern United States and along the Pacific coast, where it has been introduced, originally as a potential source of human food. Like many other amphibians, it is a carnivore, and its large size (up to eight inches; 20 cm) enables it to take a very wide range of prey, from other frogs and small fish to crayfish and even small birds.

Many frogs are very vocal in their behavior, and some, such as the carpenter frog (*Rana virgatipes*), make noises that one would not associate with amphibians. The carpenter frog, which is found in eastern bog pools surrounded by sphagnum mosses, makes a regular knocking sound, like a hammer striking wood. The northern leopard frog (*Rana pipiens*), on the other hand, makes a noise that resembles snoring. North American wetlands are quite rich in frogs, with about 12 species present, but these amphibians become even more abundant farther south in Central and South America. The northeastern regions of South America, for example, have more than 80 species of frogs. The range of living things often becomes more diverse as one passes from the temperate regions to the Tropics, and frogs illustrate this principle well.

Newts and salamanders are also important representatives of the amphibians in the wetland ecosystem. Newts, like toads, exude an unpleasant-tasting substance from their skin, so many predators avoid them. Fish eat their eggs, however, so they are vulnerable at this stage in their lives. Newts feed on insects, worms, and other small creatures, and although they spend the breeding season in and around water, they may wander far from the wetland once their eggs are laid. Like frogs, newts undergo a larval stage in their life cycle as tadpoles, when they have external gills and live as entirely aquatic animals. A newt eventually develops legs and lungs and transfers to a life above water as it reaches adulthood.

Reptiles differ from amphibians in laying eggs with shells, which makes them less dependent on water during their breeding. There are, however, many reptiles that have taken to an aquatic life in wetlands. Among the best-known wetland reptiles in North America is the snapping turtle (*Chelydra serpentine*). As its name implies, this reptile has a vicious bite and can prey upon a range of other animals, from fish to birds, but it also eats vegetation. The stinkpot, or musk turtle (*Sternotherus odoratus*), defends itself by releasing a smelly fluid when attacked. It nests on the land, as do all turtles, digging out a hollow, often under an old tree stump, and laying up to nine white eggs within it. When the eggs hatch, the young turtles are small versions of the adults; there is no larval stage as with amphibians.

Wetlands are home to many species of snakes, and all swim very well. Most water snakes swim with the characteristic sinuous rippling motion of their body, but the eastern ribbon snake (*Thamnophis sauritus*) glides over the surface of the water. The cottonmouth (*Agkistrodon piscivorus*), on the other hand, holds its head well above the water when swimming. This is the most poisonous of the wetland snakes of North America, and its bite can be fatal. Most snakes lay eggs in the same way as turtles, but the cottonmouth bears up to 15 live young. The mud snake (*Farancia abacura*) of swamps and marshes lays up to 100 eggs in a season. The female lays these in a hole in the ground and stands guard over the brood, but, as with turtles, there is no incubation by the parent because reptiles are cold-blooded, so they cannot assist in the development of the embryos. The warmth of decaying vegetation and the sunshine eventually leads the eggs to hatch, which may take up to eight weeks. The high numbers of eggs laid reflects the very high levels of predation faced by the young snakes. They are eaten by fish, amphibians, and birds, and very few survive to maturity.

Tropical wetland snakes can be large and dangerous. The Indian python (*Python molurus*) can grow to 20 feet (6 m) in length and can climb trees, so it presents a threat to the eggs and young of tree-nesting wetland birds, such as herons and egrets. The anaconda (*Eunectes murinus*) of the Amazonian wetlands is even bigger, with a length of up to 40 feet (12 m). Records of these giant reptiles eating humans are very difficult to prove and are probably exaggerated, but they can certainly handle large prey animals, such as capybara.

The most impressive group of wetland reptiles is undoubtedly the crocodilians, including the crocodiles, alligators, and caimans. Not only does this group contain the largest of living reptiles, but it also boasts the top carnivore of the food web. The American crocodile (*Crocodylus acutus*) can reach 15 feet (4.6 m) in length, and the American alligator (*Alligator mississippiensis*) is even bigger, up to 19 feet (5.8 m). The alligator has a rounded snout with no teeth visible when the mouth is closed, while the crocodile has a more slender snout and one of its teeth is visible even when the mouth is closed. The crocodile is confined to the southern tip of Florida, while the alligator is more widespread through the southern and southeastern states. The alligator builds a nest in the form of a mound of dead vegetation and lays up to 60 eggs within it. The female helps the young to excavate their way out of the nest and then continues to care for them as they mature, sometimes for several years. Alligators are important members of the wetland ecosystem, not only by operating as top carnivores but also in their role as ecosystem engineers. This is a term ecologists use to describe animals that alter the structure of their habitat such that other species benefit. The alligators' feat of engineering is to excavate holes in the mud of marshes and swamps, especially in times of drought, thus maintaining some open water. In this way they diversify the habitat and open up areas for a range of other organisms, including fish, insects, and birds.

There are 13 different species of crocodile in the world, one of the most famous being the Nile crocodile (*Crocodylus niloticus*) of Egypt. During the times of the pharaohs it was found throughout the Nile valley, but this reptile has been relentlessly hunted and is now found only upriver of Aswan, the city to the south of the Aswan High Dam, which now controls the Nile floods. It still occurs widely in eastern Africa and in isolated locations in the west. A young Nile crocodile eats mainly insects and worms, but as it grows it takes turtles, waterfowl, and mammals. It catches its prey by lying beneath the surface in waterholes and attacking animals that enter the water to drink. It often basks on land and is surprisingly agile and speedy even when out of the water.

Birds of the wetlands

There are many opportunities for birds to exploit wetlands for food and for breeding sites, and it is not surprising that wetlands provide one of the richest habitats for this group of creatures. Food for birds, whether plant or animal, is available both above and below the water surface, and different birds have adopted different methods for food collection. In deeper water birds must dive for food, and they can do this either by floating on the surface and then swimming underwater, or by diving from flight. Many ducks and also the coots and grebes adopt the first method and are able to use either their wings or their webbed feet to propel themselves in underwater swimming. Different species can dive to varying depths to obtain their food. Coots (*Fulica americana*), for example, prefer fairly shallow water, usually less than six feet (2 m) in depth. They swim on the surface, then leap into the air as they dive, tightening the feathers around their bodies to squeeze out the air layer, which would give them too much buoyancy in the water and make diving difficult. They then swim down through the water, using their feet, which are not completely webbed but have lobes of webbing along the toes. Once they reach the bottom, coots feed mainly on aquatic vegetation, although they will take invertebrate animals and small fish when these are available. Their beaks are quite short and stubby, so they are not well adapted for catching larger fish.

Grebes are much better at catching fish with their sharply pointed bills and their streamlined body shape, which allows them to swim faster and with greater ability to twist and turn underwater. Grebes have feet similar to those of coots, with only partial webbing, but their legs are set very far back on their bodies. As a result, they are quite ungainly when walking on land but extremely agile when submerged. It is this unusual structure that allows species such as the western grebe (*Aechmophorus occidentalis*) to stand almost upright in the water and skate along the surface in pairs when they are conducting their mating ceremonies. Mergansers (*Mergus merganser*) have a similar degree of maneuverability and are able to chase fish underwater, concentrating on small fish of about three to four inches (8 to 10 cm) in length. One of the real experts when it comes to diving is the goldeneye (*Bucephala clangula*). This duck can stay under water for 20 seconds or more and prefers to hunt in water that is about 12 feet (4 m) deep. It swims along the bottom and forages by turning over stones and stirring up the mud as it seeks its invertebrate prey.

The alternative way for birds to hunt in the underwater realm is to fly above the water and dive from a height, when their force as they hit the water carries them deep enough to hunt the fish upon which they prey. Forster's tern (*Sterna forsteri*) is a graceful bird with white and pearly gray plumage that employs this technique of fishing. It flies well above the water surface, with its spearlike bill pointed downward until it spots a shoal of minnows in the shallows. It is then able to hover for a moment above them before it closes its wings and drops into the water with such force that it becomes completely submerged. Holding a minnow in its bill, it then recovers and takes to flight, shaking the water from its feathers to reduce its weight when airborne. Other birds concentrate on the bigger fish, and among these none is more impressive than the osprey (*Pandion haliaetus*) in its fishing methods. This white-and-brown eagle-sized bird flies high above the water and plunges feet first upon any large fish that is basking near the surface. Its sharp talons grip the slippery prey, and its strong wing beats allow it to lift clear of the water, holding a heavy, wriggling trout or bass. Only a very powerful bird could lift such weight into the air while the heavy fish still struggles for its freedom. Bald eagles (*Haliaeetus leucocephalus*) are not great fishers. They are usually content to feed on dead fish that are washed up on the shores, or on fish they steal from ospreys by bullying them in the air. The African fish eagle (*Haliaeetus vocifer*), on the other hand, which closely resembles the bald eagle in appearance, is an expert at catching fish, using a similar plunging technique to that of the osprey.

The kingfishers are among the most brightly colored birds of the wetlands. These are also birds that use a diving technique to catch their fish. Some, like the belted kingfisher (*Ceryle alcyon*), hunt from an overhanging branch of a tree; the bird waits until a small fish passes by, when it drops headfirst into the water and catches it with its long, pointed bill. The small Eurasian kingfisher (*Alcedo atthis*) can drop from a high branch and penetrate as deep as three feet (1 m) into the water. Other kingfishers, like the pied kingfisher (*Ceryle rudis*) of Africa and Asia, hover above the water when they spot their prey. They may begin the hunt at a height of about 30 feet (10 m) above the water, and then drop in stages until they are sure of a catch before they finally take the plunge.

In very shallow water, diving and swimming underwater are not necessary. Here floating birds are able to obtain food from the bottom simply by upending and foraging in the mud while keeping their tails above water. This method of feeding is called *dabbling*. There are many species of dabbling ducks, including the common mallard (*Anas platyrhynchos*), black duck (*Anas rubripes*), blue-winged teal (*Anas discors*), American wigeon (*Anas americana*), and gadwall (*Anas strepera*). Geese and swans also feed by upending and dabbling in the shallows. The surface-feeding ducks, geese, and swans are also very prepared to climb out onto banks and drier regions of wetlands to feed. Many graze on the vegetation in such areas, and when the flocks of wildfowl are large, they can have a considerable effect on these habitats. Not only do they remove large quantities of biomass, but they are also selective in what they eat, preferring some plants to others. Canada geese (*Branta canadensis*), for example, dislike daisies. Daisies often become more abundant when geese have been grazing intensively in a grassland area because the geese have avoided the daisies and have removed grasses and other plant competitors from around them.

Pelicans have a number of fishing methods. Brown pelicans (*Pelecanus occidentalis*) use spectacular dives from flight in their hunting, while white pelicans (*Pelecanus erythrorhnchos*) hunt in groups from the surface of the water and do not dive. Cooperative hunting is quite rare among birds, but white pelicans have developed a team method in which an arc of birds thrashes the surface of the water with their wings, driving the fish together into tight groups, where they can be more easily captured.

A number of wetland birds combine an aquatic with a terrestrial way of life, inhibiting the edges of reed beds and shallow waters. They are equally at home floating on the water or running among the reeds. The moorhen (*Gallinula chloropus*) is perhaps the most familiar of this group of birds and is also undoubtedly one of the most successful in exploiting this way of life. It is a member of the rail family, but unlike the other members, including sora rail (*Porzana carolina*), Virginia rail (*Rallus limicola*), and yellow rail (*Coturnicops noveboracensis*), it is not particularly secretive. Its feet are not webbed, but its toes are long and support it as it moves over soft surfaces and floating vegetation. Its most characteristic feature is its tail, which it keeps flicking to reveal the white patches below. Even more adept at walking on floating leaves is the northern jacana (*Jacana spinosa*), which has extremely long legs and large feet that are entirely out of proportion to the rest of the body. It is found in Central America, but related jacanas are found throughout the world's tropical areas.

Another strategy for fishing in the shallows is that adopted by the herons and egrets. All these birds have long legs and long bills, and they hunt by wading through the shallow water or by standing still and waiting for a frog or a fish to

Gray heron (Ardea cinerea) *catching a fish in a Polish wetland. The spear-shaped bill of herons is ideal for catching fish and amphibians.* (Courtesy of Klaus Natura/ Minden Pictures)

pass their way. They then jab at their prey with lightning speed and grip it tightly in their bills. They twist it around until it is facing their throats and then swallow it whole. Although fish and amphibians are the favorite food of most herons, they will also take young birds and small mammals when these are available. The great blue heron (*Ardea herodias*), which is the largest of the North American heron species, is capable of killing and swallowing whole an entire adult rabbit.

Dense reed beds and cattail marshes have a vertical structure that offers opportunities for smaller birds to make a living. The common yellowthroat (*Geothlypis trichas*) is a characteristic bird of these habitats, nesting in the reeds close to the ground in drier spots. The red-winged blackbird (*Agelaius phoeniceus*) also prefers marshes and willow scrub in wetlands, as does the yellow-headed blackbird (*Xanthocephalus xanthocephalus*), which weaves its nest to stems of cattails and reeds. The European reed warbler (*Acrocephalus scirpaceus*) also uses the reeds as a nesting place, and it must weave its nest deep to ensure that eggs and young are not ejected when the reeds bend in high winds. Insect food is plentiful among the reeds; even in winter the dead vegetation beneath the reedbed cover may still harbor hibernating insects. The fruiting heads of the reeds also provide food for seed-eating species.

Predatory birds hunt the reed beds for mammals and other birds that shelter there. The northern harrier (*Circus cyaneus*), formerly known as the marsh hawk, hunts over reed beds, patrolling the area back and forth until it spots a vole or a frog, when it drops among the reeds on folded wings. In Europe the larger marsh harrier (*Circus aeruginosus*) will take ducks from the surface of the water, hitting them with its talons and carrying them off in flight. The snail kite (*Rostrhamus sociabilis*) of the Florida Everglades has an extremely long and curved upper mandible to its beak. It feeds on snails that climb the stems of reeds in the marshes, picking them off in flight and then extracting them from the shells with its curved and sharply pointed bill.

Forested wetlands are rich in woodpecker species that take advantage of dead and dying trees to construct their nest holes and to seek their insect prey. One such is the hoatzin (*Opisthocomus hoazin*), which lives in the tropical forested wetlands of the Amazon. This is not a particularly attractive bird, having the general appearance of a scruffy chicken with a bristly crest. It spends most of its time scrambling around in the branches of trees, eating flowers, fruits, and foliage. The hoatzin is not fond of flying, and it sometimes consumes so much vegetable matter that it falls off its branch into the water. It is able to swim quite well, however, and soon scrambles out and climbs a tree once more. The hoatzin's most remarkable feature is found in the young birds, which have two claws present on the main joint of the wing, giving them an improved ability to hang onto the tree branches and thus avoid becoming the prey of the caimans and piranhas in the water beneath.

Spoonbills are found in tropical and temperate wetlands. The roseate spoonbill is the only example found in North

America, but it is also one of the most brightly colored of the group. As its name implies, the bill is spoon-shaped, or *spatulate,* and the broad tip is well adapted to sieving microscopic food from the water.

The northern bogs and tundra mires are the breeding grounds for many species of wading birds. These have long legs and long bills and are adapted for probing into the soft mud and peat of the bog habitat. Some, like the marbled godwit (*Limosa fedoa*), spend their winter in coastal wetlands and then migrate to the prairie mires to breed, while others, such as the short-billed dowitcher (*Limnodromus griseus*) and the greater yellowlegs (*Tringa melanoleuca*), move farther north to the boreal wetlands and open Arctic muskeg mires for their nesting activities. The greater yellowlegs prefers bogs that have scattered trees, such as tamarack, and uses these to perch and watch out for approaching predators. Many of the smaller waders, however, including least sandpipers (*Calidris minutilla*) and dunlin (*Calidris alpina*), prefer the wetland regions beyond the forest limits and breed on bleak and open tundra mires.

Roseate spoonbill (Ajaja ajaja) in its full breeding plumage. Found in the southern United States, this spectacular bird feeds by sieving tiny animals from muddy water by means of its flattened bill. (Courtesy of Tim Fitzharris/ Minden Pictures)

Mammals of the wetlands

Many mammals have adopted an aquatic existence and have taken to the wetlands. Perhaps the most widely known wetland mammal is the beaver (*Castor canadensis*), which is found throughout the northern regions of the world, except where it has been exterminated by humans. It prefers forested wetlands because it feeds upon twigs and branches of a number of different trees, and it also uses trees to construct its own wetland habitat. It can be regarded as an ecosystem engineer, deliberately manipulating the environment to suit its own particular needs. The beaver constructs dams across wetland streams by felling small trees with its sharp, chisel-like teeth, and it interweaves these in such a way as to raise the level of water and flood surrounding forest. Dams may be as long as 1,000 yards (1 km) and as much as 10 feet (3 m) high. Trees upstream of the dam may die as a result of the flooding and the spread of the wetland habitat. With webbed feet and a flat, rudderlike tail beavers are expert swimmers, so they take advantage of the open-water areas that they produce, swimming up the flooded valleys of tributary streams and gaining water access deeper into the forest.

In the lake behind their dam beavers construct a lodge (see the illustration), which consists of a pile of interwoven sticks that rises above water level but has underwater entrances. Here the beaver is safe from most predators, including lynx, wolf, and bear, and is also protected from the worst of the winter cold. The lodge can be up to 20 feet (7 m) in diameter and may contain several rooms. It is occupied by an entire beaver family with as many as 10 members. When winter is approaching, the beavers stockpile twigs and bark in the lodge as food for the winter. This material is stored under the water, where the frozen surface keeps it fresh.

To the north of the boreal forests where the beaver lives, the Arctic mires support herds of grazing caribou (*Rangifer tarandus*). These large deer have broad hooves with concave undersides that support their weight when walking across soft wetland surfaces. They feed upon the fresh growth of vegetation in the spring and resort to lichens in the harsh winter months. By migrating south over the tundra regions, they manage to avoid the worst of the winter cold. Other

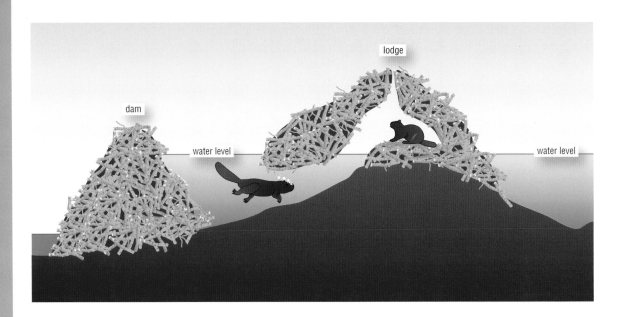

Cross section of a beaver dam and lodge. The lodge is entered by means of an underwater passage.

species of deer graze the vegetation in the boreal mires of the forested region, elk (*Cervus elaphus*) and moose (*Alces alces*) being the chief among these. The moose is particularly fond of spending its summer months wading in shallow-water wetlands within the coniferous forest, where it grazes on submerged vegetation. These aquatic plants are rich in certain elements, including sodium, which the moose needs and which are generally scarce in this environment.

In southern Asia the main large mammalian herbivore of wetlands is the water buffalo (*Bubalus arnee*). This animal has been domesticated for the past 2,500 years in northern India and Burma. It is a placid beast that is happy wading up to its shoulders in water and eating the aquatic vegetation. Its main predator in the wild is the tiger (*Panthera tigris*), which is the largest of all mammalian wetland predators. Whereas lions avoid water, tigers are at home in wetland habitats and can swim strongly. The coastal wetlands of Bangladesh remain one of the few strongholds of the tiger in the wild.

In the Amazon wetlands the chief mammalian grazer is a rodent, the capybara (*Hydrochoerus hydrochaeris*). This is the largest of all rodents, being about the size of a sheep. It is around four feet (1.3 m) in length and is remarkable in having webbed feet. Its feet allow it to walk over soft ground and also to swim in water. It is vegetarian and, like all rodents, has long incisor teeth that keep growing through its entire life, being continuously worn down by constant grazing. The capybara is a social animal, living in groups of about 20 individuals, which may help to alert it to the presence of its predators. These include the jaguar (*Panthera onca*) on land and the caiman in the water. The coypu (*Myocastor coypus*), or nutria, is another South American rodent living in the wetlands. It is a marsh and reed bed dweller, feeding upon the shoots of reeds around the edges of water. Like the capybara, it swims readily, but it is a smaller animal, rarely exceeding two feet (60 cm) in length. Its fur consists of two layers, the outer being coarse and bristly and the inner soft and fleecy. This enables it to stay dry even after spending long periods in the water. These properties have made the fur very attractive to the clothing industry, and coypus have been farmed for fur production in Europe, Russia, and North America. At times captive coypu have escaped and established themselves in the wild, sometimes becoming a pest because of their destructive activities in riverbanks and in reed beds. In England, for example, a large wild population became established but it has now been eradicated by a program of trapping.

The marshes of Africa are grazed by several large mammal species including the reedbuck (*Redunca arundinum*), kob (*Kobus kob*), waterbuck (*Kobus ellipsiprymnus*), and the lechwe (*Kobus leche*). The waterbuck has a distinctively greasy appearance and also a smell that can be detected even by the insensitive noses of humans at a range of a quarter mile. It rarely strays from marshes and grazes on the reeds that shelter it. The very high productivity of reed beds in the Tropics of Africa means that dense populations of waterbuck can be supported, sometimes reaching 250 per square mile (1,000 per square kilometer). They are territorial animals, the males fighting off other males and attracting breeding females into their territories. The lechwe is another antelope of southern African wetlands that spends much of its time wading in water up to three feet (1 m) deep. It is able to avoid some of its predators by taking to the water, but even lions will sometimes follow it into the marsh, and there is always the possibility that crocodiles will be waiting in the open water, so wetlands are not an entirely safe haven.

Some relatives of humans, the primates, occupy wetlands, including the chimpanzee (*Pan troglodytes*), which will wade through water, holding its arms above its head in a very humanlike stance. In the mangrove swamps of southern Asia, the proboscis monkey (*Nasalis larvatus*) is a characteristic canopy dweller, eating fruit and using the upper branches of the mangal trees to escape the attentions of its main predator, the tiger. The orangutan (*Pongo pygmaeus*) is the largest wetland primate, occupying the coastal swamp forests of southeast Asia (see "Different kinds of wetlands," pages 10–37). Its strange name is derived from the Malay language, *orang* meaning "man," and *utan* meaning "jungle." It is a massive primate, males weighing up to 220 pounds (100 kg) and females up to 100 pounds (45 kg). It has long arms, with a span of up to eight feet (2.4 m), but quite short legs. The arms are the orangutan's main means of locomotion as it moves through the forest canopy above the wet forest floor. It is an herbivore and has a very wide range of food options, from fruit and leaves to bark and roots. It is even willing to consume humus and developing peat from the forest floor. Orangutans make nests in the trees where they sleep, but when a cave is available they have been known to make use of these more solid shelters. This close relative of humans has become endangered mainly because of human hunting, but now the destruction of its wetland forests is its greatest threat.

Conclusions

Living in a wetland presents many challenges to plants and animals. Lack of oxygen is a serious problem for animals living in the mud at the base of wetlands because oxygen diffuses so much more slowly through water than in air. Many aquatic invertebrate animals have developed special breathing organs, and microbes have a range of biochemical adaptations that enable them to cope with the low oxygen concentrations. Plant roots also have difficulty in obtaining sufficient oxygen, and adaptations for the transport of air down hollow stems and leaf stalks are found in some floating and emergent aquatic plants. The chemical conditions of wetlands can also place stresses upon animals, especially extreme acidity; in such acidic conditions some elements, such as aluminum, may be present at levels that are toxic and others, such as calcium, may be in very short supply.

Despite these problems, or perhaps in part because of them, the life of wetlands has evolved in a great variety of forms. Wetlands are among the most diverse ecosystems on Earth, and this biodiversity is found in all the major groups of plants and animals. The plants of wetlands include submerged and floating aquatic species and emergent plants, which hold their shoots or leaves above the surface of the water. These emergents, including cattails and reeds, create a structure above the water in which many animals are able to make a living. Some trees can tolerate wet soils, and these provide an even more complex architecture in which animals thrive. But some lowly plants are very influential in wetland development, including the bog mosses, genus *Sphagnum*, which can convert wetland forest into open bog landscapes. On the acidic raised masses of peat that develop from sphagnum communities, the only plants that can survive have adaptations to the acid, low-fertility environment. The most highly adapted of these are the carnivorous plants, which consume insects as a means of supplementing their nitrogen intake and protein production.

There is an unseen, microscopic biodiversity within the waters of all wetlands, including primary producers, such as the phytoplankton and algae; consumers, such as the ciliates and microscopic crustaceans; and detritivores, such as the amoebas. Small fish, crustaceans, amphibians, and reptiles take their energy from this microscopic food web and build upon it to form a resource of food for larger organisms, such as the frogs, snakes, and bird life of the reed beds, swamps, and bogs.

Among the birds of wetlands, there are many feeding strategies. Some dive into water for their food, either from the air or from the water surface, while others dabble at the edges, feeding upon the bottom-dwelling organisms. Some birds spend their time along the edges of the reed beds, gathering

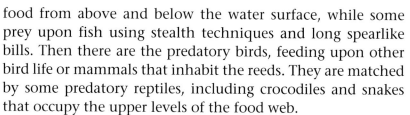

food from above and below the water surface, while some prey upon fish using stealth techniques and long spearlike bills. Then there are the predatory birds, feeding upon other bird life or mammals that inhabit the reeds. They are matched by some predatory reptiles, including crocodiles and snakes that occupy the upper levels of the food web.

Mammals play many roles in the wetlands. Some of the large grazing animals of wetlands are mammals, including many species of deer, from the caribou of the north to the waterbuck and lechwe of the tropical marshes. In South America rodents are the main large grazers. In Southeast Asia primates can also play an important grazing role in the community. Some of the top carnivores of wetlands are also mammals, including the tiger and jaguar. The biodiversity of wetlands, therefore, contains contributions from a wide range of plant and animal groups.

CHAPTER 5

WETLANDS IN HISTORY

Wetlands are far older than the human species. As *Homo sapiens* began to spread over the face of the Earth, wetlands were part of the environment encountered. No doubt they were initially a barrier to human spread, but once people had mastered the art of boat building, what was once a barrier became a highway, a means of rapid travel and exploration. One of the features that have made humans so successful is adaptability, and wetlands were early recognized as productive habitats, rich in food resources. Our hunter-gatherer ancestors exploited the wetlands and often placed their dwellings around their edges as they developed a fishing economy. But wetlands also brought their dangers in the form of floods and disease, so wetlands have historically been a source of both joy and of despair, a fact that is reflected in art and literature.

Prehistoric people of the wetlands

Chapter 2 described how wetlands record their own history in their layered sediments and how plant and animal remains are preserved in lake mud and bog peat. This is true not only for the wetland plants and animals but also for the remains of humans and their tools and buildings when these were located in a wetland setting. In dry land archaeological excavations only the most robust material survives in the soil, including bones, stone implements, and pottery. However, in wetland sites much more is preserved; wood, skin, hair, and the remains of food may all survive and provide evidence of former lifestyles, leading to the development of a distinct discipline of wetland archaeology.

The success of wetland archaeology depends upon the presence of human activities and settlements in areas that are now buried by wetland sediments, and one area where this has commonly taken place is in northwest Europe. This is an area that saw considerable prehistoric settlement and also experienced changes in sea level that created and preserved ancient wetlands. At the end of the last glaciation, the coastline of Europe looked very different from that of the present day because the British Isles were then a part of mainland Europe. The sea level at the end of the last glaciation was more than 300 feet (100 m) lower than at present because so much of the world's water was locked up in major ice sheets over areas of Europe, Asia, and North America. As the climate became warmer beginning around 13,000 years ago, world sea levels began to rise. Large areas of northern Europe were low-lying and were occupied by extensive wetlands, and these were gradually lost as the sea rose and flooded them, eventually separating Ireland from Britain and Britain from the continental mainland. Beneath the shallow waters of the North Sea there now lie peat deposits from the wetlands of ancient times, and some of these deposits have yielded archaeological remains showing that people once lived and hunted in these lost lands.

Fishing boats trawling their nets on the floor of the North Sea have occasionally collected lumps of peat containing prehistoric tools, including a barbed harpoon made of bone that dates from more than 8,000 years ago. One can conclude that people belonging to the Middle Stone Age (Mesolithic) culture were freely crossing the wetlands that are now submerged and were fishing in their waters with harpoons. Around the edges of the coastlines even more archaeological discoveries have been made. Off the east coast of England an exceptionally low tide revealed a circle of upright tree trunks that provide evidence of a prehistoric religious site constructed from timber. Stone circles of this kind are well known in Europe, dating from between 3,000 and 5,000 years ago, but this discovery suggests that wooden equivalents may have been widely used but have been lost in all but the wetland sites.

Many peat deposits lie submerged between Ireland and Wales in the west of Britain, including some remarkable trackways laid down about 4,000 years ago by people who regularly walked across the wetlands and who were likely troubled by the rising water levels. They cut the stems of hazel and other trees and laid them in carefully constructed walking tracks so that they could continue to cross the wetlands on foot in their hunting activities. Settlements on the coast have also been discovered that are now buried in peat, including one from 10,000 years ago in which the foundations of wooden huts and jetties can still be seen and where the remains of deer, moose, wild pigs, and wild cattle provide evidence of their main prey animals. The presence of waterfowl remains, including those of ducks, grebes, cranes, and storks, shows that they were exploiting the local wetland as a source of food.

Lakeside settlements from prehistoric times in Europe are also known. In Switzerland and northern Italy the remains of whole wetland villages, raised on stilts above the water, have been excavated. At one site in Poland, called Biskupin, a very large lakeside settlement with rows of terraced wooden dwellings dating from more than 2,000 years ago has been found, and the history and decline of this site has been reconstructed in some detail (see the photo on page 132). The large town was built entirely of timber and was heavily fortified against neighboring tribes by a massive stockade built around its perimeter, together with tall watchtowers and gatehouses. Within the town the rows of houses were also built of wood, and it is likely that the surrounding landscape must have been stripped of its forest to provide the timber for the site. Archaeologists have calculated that 35,000 oak and pine trees must have been felled to complete this construction. However, the removal of such extensive areas of timber had devastating consequences. Trees take up water from the soil and lose it to the atmosphere through their leaves. When people remove trees from a landscape, more water passes through the soil into valley streams and lakes. The loss of trees at Biskupin resulted in an excess of floodwater draining into the wetlands that bordered the town and had protected it from attack on one side. As the water level rose, the town became flooded and had to be abandoned, so the wetland took over and the collapsing timbers became buried in accumulating peat. Now the town has been excavated once more, and the ancient walls and buildings have been reconstructed from timber according to the original layout of the streets. The peat, rather like the volcanic ash at the ancient Roman city of Pompeii, has preserved an entire culture and way of life beneath its layers.

In North America the remains of fortified islands and peninsulas have been discovered that provide some information about settlements of Native American peoples on the edges of wetlands, but the scale of these settlements is not as great as that of the European sites. In the northwest, settlements were present around Vancouver Island that date back 3,000 years. Villages on the edge of wetlands clearly depended on fishing for their food. The salmon run in Puget Sound was being exploited even in those days, but local people also collected shellfish and stored them in baskets made of tree bark. Wood carvings have also been collected from this area, some of which have been decorated with the teeth of sea otters. The Florida wetlands offer great opportunities

Biskupin in Poland was an Iron Age settlement on the edge of a lake. The timber village has been reconstructed on the basis of wood foundations preserved in the lake sediments.
(Courtesy of Peter D. Moore)

for the development of this type of archaeology in the future.

In New Zealand some work has been done on wetland settlements of early Maori people dating from before the arrival of European explorers. They show that groups of up to about 30 people probably lived together in fortified villages, usually consisting of five houses.

Human remains have also been found in peat deposits. Cemeteries for the disposal of the dead were normally constructed on dry land, however, so the bodies that have been discovered in the bogs are unlikely to represent the normal means of burial. Another factor also suggests that these were not normal interments. There is often evidence of a violent death, such as a rope around the neck or a sinister fracture of the skull. The relative frequency of the finds of human bodies in peat lands, especially in Ireland, England, and Denmark, and often dating from 2,000 to 2,500 years ago, suggests that these were not just casual murders but were ritual sacrifices. Perhaps they were criminals who were executed and then offered as a sacrifice to some wetland deity. One or two even appear to have been pegged to the surface of the peat and left there to die.

What is most remarkable about the discovery of intact human remains in wetland sediments is the extraordinary degree of preservation of features of the skin and hair, together with the clothing fabrics that covered them. In acid peat the bones are dissolved, but the proteins of skin, fingernails, and hair are perfectly preserved so that even fingerprints could quite easily be taken. The contents of the stomachs are also well preserved, so it is possible to determine what constituted the victim's last meal. Wetland archaeology can thus give us a rare glimpse into the way of life of our ancestors.

Wetlands may have provided many opportunities for hunters and food gatherers, but they proved of little use for agriculture. There are some crops that enjoy a wet soil, such as rice, the North American wild rice, and the European water chestnut, but the advent of agriculture caused a change in the status of wetlands as far as humans were concerned. The new crops, including wheat, barley, and oats, came from the Middle East. They were dry-habitat crops, and the extension of agriculture demanded the drainage of wet soils, so human relationships with wetlands swung in a negative direction, and thus it has remained up until very recent times.

Modern wetland people

Some cultures have developed alongside and even within the wetland habitats and still look to the wetlands as a source of food. In southern Iraq, the Marsh Arabs have long lived within the wetlands of the Euphrates delta, subsisting on fish and building their dwellings from reeds. Similarly, in Africa's Okavango delta the native people look to the wetlands as a source of fish and the flesh of the wetland antelope, the lechwe (see "Mammals of the wetlands," pages 123–126). About 400 tons (406 tonnes) of fish are extracted from the waters and marshes of this inland wetland each year, and the seasonally flooded regions also provide grazing for domesticated animals. These wetlands provide more than half a million acres (1.5 million ha) of grazing land. Many African communities depend upon seasonal wetlands in this way. In Sudan the Nile River passes through the great Sudd swamps, and these are the most productive ecosystems in the region. Farmers periodically move their herds of cattle, estimated at 800,000 head, into the region to supplement their grazing. The Senegal River in west Africa has wetland habitats that support even larger cattle herds, perhaps as many as 2 million, and there are another 3 million cattle grazing in the delta of the Niger River.

These wetlands also supply supplementary meat from wild herbivores, such as the lechwe in the Okavango. This supply, known as "bush meat," is important for local populations but is also a problem for conservation of wild populations if demand becomes too heavy. The people of the Sudd wetlands are thought to obtain as much as one-quarter of their protein intake from the wildlife of the region. At present the Sudd contains around half a million wild antelope, so their population is not under threat, but such hunting needs to be controlled and documented if overexploitation is to be avoided.

Perhaps some of the wetland herbivores, such as the lechwe, which are so well adapted to life in the marshes, could be managed as semidomesticated animals and thus exploit the resources of the wetlands more efficiently than cattle do.

Coastal mangrove wetlands provide a living for many different groups of people, especially in Southeast Asia, from the Sundarbans of Bangladesh to the Mekong Delta of Vietnam. These wetlands provide a harvest of fish, shrimps, and crabs as well as timber and honey. (Bees thrive in the rich swampland of the mangroves.) There is a danger, however, that people will take materials out of these ecosystems faster than they can be renewed. It takes more than 50 years for a mangrove tree to grow to a size that makes it valuable for timber, and it is nearer 160 years before it is fully mature. Timber extraction is taking place on a shorter interval than this, which will ultimately result in the degradation of this wetland habitat.

People and wetlands can coexist, but the wetland habitats are clearly under strain as human populations and food demands rise. The future of the wetlands and the wetland people they support is uncertain.

Wetlands and disease

Throughout recorded human history wetlands have been associated with disease. In the century before the birth of Christ, the Roman scholar Marcus Terentius Varro (116–28 B.C.E.) made the remarkable proposal that there were tiny disease-carrying organisms in swampy places that were too small to be seen but were carried through the air in the swamp gases and marsh mists, passing into human bodies through the nostrils and causing disease. It took almost 2,000 years for this idea to develop into a full theory of bacterial disease. Meanwhile, most people believed that it was the gases themselves that led to the development of disease among people living in the wetlands.

Of all the human diseases with wetland connections, malaria is the most widespread, affecting 500 million people worldwide. It was also one of the first diseases that was associated with wetland habitats. In the fifth century B.C.E. a man from Sicily named Empedocles (precise dates of birth and death are uncertain, but his main work was conducted around 444 B.C.E.) came up with the idea that the wetlands of that island were responsible for the frequency of "swamp fever," or malaria, in the region. He recommended the drainage of wetlands as a means of controlling the spread of malaria. The scheme worked, and a special coin was struck in honor of Empedocles and to celebrate the victory over the disease.

Malaria has distinctive symptoms: intermittent bouts of chills and fever and swelling of the liver and spleen. There was no known cure until the 18th century, when Jesuit priests returning to Europe from South America described the measures used there. They reported that the native peoples of that continent used the bark of cinchona tree (*Cinchona officianalis*) as a means of controlling the disease. Quinine, a compound that occurs naturally in cinchona bark, attacks the protozoan parasite *Plasmodium,* which occupies the blood of the sufferer during fever attacks. At the time, however, people did not understand precisely how quinine worked. The disease was considered to be a consequence of the bad air (*mal aria,* from the Italian) associated with wetlands. In 1848 an Alabama doctor, Josiah Nott, proposed that malaria was carried to humans by mosquitoes, but it took until the end of that century to reveal the complete life cycle of the malarial parasite. The protozoan parasite is taken into the mosquito with its meal of human blood from an infected individual. The parasite then reproduces within the mosquito and passes from the salivary glands of the insect into the next human it feeds upon. Within the human it resides in the liver and periodically erupts into the blood in large numbers, causing the symptoms of swamp fever.

As Empedocles had found, an alternative to treating the parasite in the sufferer is to drain the marshes that are associated with malaria. Since the discovery of mosquitoes' role in the transmission of the disease, this option has often been adopted for malaria control. People have also used pesticides as a means of attacking the mosquito directly, and the use of DDT was once thought to be the ideal way of eradicating the disease. Unfortunately, as people gradually learned, a persistent pesticide like DDT causes devastation to wildlife and eventually ends up in the bodies of human beings, so the cure in this case was as bad as the disease. Today's emphasis is upon the development of more effective drugs for the control of the parasite within the human body, but evolution takes place in the parasite almost as fast as drug development takes place in the laboratory, so strains of *Plasmodium* that are resistant to new drugs are constantly evolving. Climate change may also present new problems because the species of mosquito that acts as an intermediary host for the parasite will be able to colonize lands beyond its current range, perhaps extending into the southern United States and southern Europe.

Schistosomiasis, or bilharzia, is another tropical disease associated with wetlands. It affects around 200 million people, mainly in Africa and South America, causing excessive sweating and the passing of blood in urine. It is caused by tiny wormlike organisms that live in human blood and other tissues. The parasites become abundant in the intestines and in the wall of the bladder, where they mate and lay their eggs. The human host then sheds these eggs with feces and urine, and they enter the wetlands in regions where there is no sewage treatment. Freshwater snails eat the eggs and they hatch within the snails into larvae that are shed back into the water. There the larvae wait until they discover some unprotected skin, usually on the bare feet of people wading in the water, and they penetrate the skin and take up residence in a human once more. The records of the ancient Egyptians show that the disease was known to them. When the army of Napoleon conquered Egypt in 1798, the disease reached epidemic proportions among the soldiers. It was in Cairo in 1851 that a young German doctor, Theodor Bilharz (1825–62), discovered the organism that causes the disease, and within 60 years the entire life cycle had been worked out.

As in the case of malaria, the control of schistosomiasis has proved difficult. Treatment within the human body using drugs is an option, as is the draining of wetlands. But in countries such as Egypt the waterways are a vital part of human life, so their loss is not acceptable. An alternative is the control of the intermediate host, the snail. There are chemicals

River ghetto on the Amazon River, Iquitos, Peru. Living beside wetlands can bring risks of waterborne diseases. (Courtesy of Gerry Ellis/Minden Pictures)

now available (called molluscicidal agents) that are poisonous to the snails, but in order to be effective in the field, these must not be poisonous to humans, domestic animals, or the fish that are taken from the wetlands. One important approach to the control of the disease is education of people.

Better sanitation and waste disposal is required rather than dumping all refuse, including sewage, into the waterways. People must also beware wading in the water, which involves exposing their bare skin to the waiting parasite larvae.

Drinking water that has been contaminated with sewage is one of the most frequent means of disease spread, especially in wetland regions. Cholera is a disease long associated with the Ganges Delta in India. It is caused by a bacterium that causes intense diarrhea in the victim and is voided from the body in feces. It is then able to survive outside the human body in contaminated water, and it requires no intermediate host before invading the next person who drinks the water. Usually the monsoon rains in the Himalaya Mountains flush through the waterways of the Ganges Delta and cleanse them, but when the rains are delayed or are weaker than usual, the disease may build up in the local human populations. Periodically, epidemics develop, and these may spread with alarming speed across the continent and into other parts of the world, causing pandemics. During one outbreak in London in 1854, a young physician, John Snow (1813–58), conducted a careful analysis of the geographical locations of new cases and found that all the infected people were using water from one particular source, a public water pump. He thus concluded that contaminated drinking water was the means of spread of this disease. His findings proved of great interest in New York City, and authorities there were able to control a cholera outbreak in 1866 by isolating and cleansing drinking water sources.

Water and wetlands are thus potential sources for some very serious human diseases, especially in the Tropics but also in the temperate regions. Many wetlands have been drained in the past in the name of disease control. Fortunately, the emphasis of modern medicine has moved in the direction of more effective drug treatments for diseases, coupled with higher standards of hygiene and sewage disposal.

Exploration of the wetlands

Wetlands have played an important role in global exploration. In days before air transport, the only means of penetrating the interior of a continent was over land or by boat up the rivers. Of the two options, the latter was often preferable because heavy equipment and supplies could be more easily transported in boats than by animal-drawn carts over the land.

One of the greatest stories of exploration that the world has ever known is the search for the source of the Nile River in eastern Africa. The Nile valley formed the backdrop for one of the world's earliest civilizations in ancient Egypt, so the lower parts of this river and its delta wetlands were well known throughout history. But to the south lay lands of great mystery that were regarded as impenetrable by Western civilization. The Greek traveler Herodotus (ca. 484–c. 407 B.C.E.) had reached as far south as Aswan (see the map) in 460 B.C.E. but failed to penetrate beyond the first cataract of the Nile. Progress beyond this cataract was not possible by river but would have involved portage of the boats overland. Five hundred years later, two Roman soldiers under Emperor Nero returned from an expedition up the Nile with stories of a great impenetrable marsh. It is possible that these intrepid soldiers had gone as far as the Sudd marshes in the south of what is now Sudan. If so, they had managed remarkably well. But many rumors existed at that time, most based on imaginative speculation, although some elements subsequently proved to have a factual basis. There were stories of two great inland seas in eastern Africa and of great mountains, the so-called Mountains of the Moon, which were reputed to contain the source of the Nile River.

The interior landscape of Africa remained a mystery to the Western world until Christian missionaries began to penetrate inland from the east coast in the mid-19th century. They brought back stories of snow-capped mountains (Mount Kilimanjaro and Mount Kenya), and these tales brought the 2,000-year-old fables of the Mountains of the Moon back into the public imagination. Arab slave traders along the coast also confirmed the presence of a great inland lake, which they called Lake Nyanza (later renamed Lake Victoria), which also seemed to confirm the ancient stories of East African geography. But the serious search for the source of the Nile began in 1856, when two British explorers,

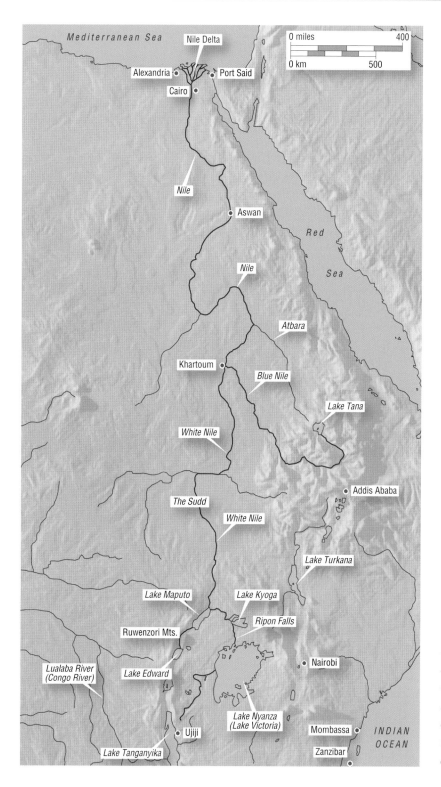

Map of East Africa, showing the Nile River and some of the locations that played an important part in the early exploration of this region

Richard Burton (1821–90) and John Speke (1827–64), set out to solve one of the greatest geographical mysteries of their time. Rather than journey south and follow the Nile over the Sudanese desert, they traveled to the east coast of Africa and journeyed overland to seek the great inland lakes. Diseased and exhausted, they eventually arrived at Lake Tanganyika and were hopeful that they might have discovered the source of the Nile. They were disappointed, however, discovering that the lake was actually at too low an elevation, sunk in the Rift Valley, to provide water for the Nile. Greatly dispirited, they began their return to the east coast, but on the way Speke left the main party and headed north to see if the fabled Lake Nyanza lay in that region. After many days trekking over dry scrubland, the landscape began to take on a moister appearance, with water holes and swamps, and eventually opened onto the vast expanse of the lake itself. Far too wide for its farther shore to be visible, its margins clothed in rich marshes of papyrus, the lake greatly excited Speke. In a moment of exhilaration he declared that this was the true source of the Nile River. He had no real evidence for this assertion, only a deep conviction that this was the case. When he later rejoined Burton, he met with a skeptical response, and the two developed a very strained relationship after this event. Perhaps it was Burton's demand for scientific proof, or perhaps there was some jealousy at Speke's discovery of the lake.

Speke returned to England, full of enthusiasm for his theory that Lake Nyanza was the source of the Nile, and he soon made plans for another expedition to search the north side of the lake for the location where the river set out on its journey toward the Mediterranean Sea. Burton was not invited to join him on this expedition. In July 1862 Speke found what he was looking for. A massive river left Lake Nyanza by way of an impressive waterfall on its northern shore, its waters heading northward toward Sudan and Egypt. The river at this stage was treacherous and inhabited by crocodiles, its banks clothed with swamps and seemingly impenetrable forest. As a result, Speke was unable to confirm his theory that this was the Nile by following it downriver to the Sudd marshes and beyond. There was thus a gap in the knowledge of the river's course, and Burton and others continued to doubt the identity of Speke's river.

On Speke's return to Britain, he and Burton were to debate the geographical evidence for the source of the Nile at a scientific convention. However, just before Speke was due to give his account of his findings he died in a hunting accident, and this tragic event threw the geographical meeting into confusion. No one has been able to establish whether the death of Speke, from a gunshot wound near his heart, was indeed an accident or was suicide prompted by his frustration in being unable to prove beyond doubt that his lake was the source of the Nile. Within a few more years, however, all the blanks on the map had been filled in, and the proof that Speke had sought had been obtained. The river flowing north out of Lake Nyanza (now Lake Victoria) was indeed the Nile; Burton was wrong and Speke had been correct all along.

Solving the problem of the Nile's origins did not close the book on the discovery of Africa's wetlands. The course of the Nile had been known in part for more than 2,000 years, but on the west coast of Africa a river emerged from the very heart of the continent that was a total mystery. That river was the Congo. In the early 19th century little was known of this river except that its mouth in the southern Atlantic Ocean was choked with masses of mangrove wetlands. Its banks were obscured by a tangle of jungle growth, hindering systematic exploration, yet the American journalist Henry Morton Stanley (1841–1904) undertook to explore the Congo River. His story is intricately connected with that of a Scottish missionary, David Livingstone (1813–73), who set out for Africa's interior and explored its wetlands from the east coast of the continent.

Livingstone set off for Africa in 1865, and one of his main concerns remained the source of the Nile, still in dispute following Speke's untimely death. He had already spent much time in Africa, and had followed the Zambesi River and become the first European to see Victoria Falls. On this later journey he followed the original Burton/Speke trail west to Lake Tanganyika. Livingstone then continued westward, beyond the lake, and came upon a northward-running river that he firmly believed to be the Nile. In fact, he had discovered the headwaters of the Congo. Sick and exhausted, he returned to Lake Tanganyika and rested in the village of Ujiji.

Back in Britain, Livingstone was feared dead because no news of him had emerged from Africa for several years. African exploration generated as much excitement and media attention in the 19th century as space travel did in the 20th century, and the general public were eager to discover more about the fate of the Scottish missionary in the dark forests of Africa. As a consequence, the editor of the New York *Herald,* James Gordon Bennett Jr. (1841–1918), financed an expedition to seek the lost missionary. It was to be led by Henry Morton Stanley. Stanley was originally a Welshman and had changed his name from Rowlands. He had gained a reputation as a journalist during the American Civil War and had subsequently become an American citizen. He now followed the trail Livingstone had taken, heading into the heart of Africa from the east coast. In his account of the journey, recorded in his best-selling book *How I Found Livingstone in Central Africa,* he described in vivid detail the hardships of his journey. Wading through crocodile-infested, neck-deep swamps and constantly afflicted by malaria, he made his way westward toward Lake Tanganyika. The story of his entry into the village of Ujiji and his meeting with Livingstone has become one of the best-known events in the history of African exploration. On meeting the first white man he had set eyes on for many months, here in the most remote region of Central Africa, he made the quaint observation, "Dr. Livingstone, I presume?" Such a simple remark ensured the immortality of this pioneer journalist.

Stanley's success in this project and his consequent fame and popular acclaim brought him personal fame and fortune. In 1874 he returned to Africa and circumnavigated Lake Victoria, confirming the great river that Speke had described leaving its northern shore. He was cautious, however, about asserting that this was the source of the Nile because he was still intrigued by the northward-flowing river that Livingstone had found to the west of Lake Tanganyika. Heading west from Lake Victoria, Stanley found the Ruwenzori Mountains and identified these with the Mountains of the Moon that had been a source of speculation for 2,000 years. He made his way back to the village of Ujiji and retraced the tracks of Livingstone to the river he had described. There was only one way to check on the identity of the river; if it was indeed the Nile, then it would eventually lead to the Mediterranean Sea. So off he set with his expedition to follow the course of Livingstone's river. His story of this journey is extremely harrowing. He was attacked by tribes and had all his supplies and medicines stolen. He was shipwrecked and plagued by sickness. Of the 356 men who set out on the journey, only 114 remained alive at the end, and Stanley had the good fortune to be one of these. Three years after leaving the east coast of Africa, the decimated and bedraggled party found themselves in a network of mangrove islands and river channels that proved to be the mouth of the Congo on the west coast of Africa. Livingstone's river was not the Nile, but the outcome of the expedition was just as exciting and informative about the geography of Africa. Stanley had traced the full course of the Congo River and in doing so had become the first person to cross the entire African continent. The regions he had passed through—the marshes of Lake Victoria, the high-altitude bogs of the Ruwenzori Mountains, the forested swamps of the upper Congo River, and the mangrove vegetation of its delta—contained some of the richest and most diverse wetlands in the world.

Africa was not the only continent in which wetland exploration and discovery was taking place. In South America another great river and wetland system lay beyond the knowledge of the developing world, the Amazon River. As in the case of the Congo River, the mouth of the Amazon on the western edge of the South Atlantic Ocean had been known to sailors for some time. Spanish sailors, some of whom had first sailed with Columbus, recorded the extensive delta of the Amazon and conjectured that it led to a great inland sea. But the full course of the Amazon was documented almost by accident. During the Spanish conquest of South America, soldiers concentrated their activity in the western mountain chain, the Andes Mountains, where they hoped to find the fabled city of El Dorado with its gold and riches. One expedition that had set out to seek this city, under the leadership of Gonzalo

Pizarro (1502?–48) in 1541, became lost and entangled in the jungles of the Andes foothills. Provisions were almost exhausted and the expedition split into two parties. One under Pizarro's leadership set off on foot to try to reach Ecuador, while the other, led by a man called Francisco de Orellana (ca. 1490–ca. 1546), built a boat and embarked on an easterly journey down one of the rivers leading out of the mountains. Pizarro's party eventually reached safety, but there was no news of Orellana, and it was feared that his group was lost. In fact, Orellana had experienced many problems in their journey downriver, mainly from battles with neighboring tribes. One attack that left a deep impression on the Spanish soldiers was reportedly carried out entirely by a party of naked warrior women. Recollecting the classical Greek tale of Hercules and his encounter with a tribe of female warriors, the Spaniards called their attackers "Amazons," and this word persisted as the name of the river down which they traveled. Orellana eventually reached the Atlantic Ocean and made his way to the Caribbean, having completed a remarkable journey of exploration. The origin and the course of the Amazon were thus known long before those of the Nile or the Congo.

In North America the first European settlement took place along the eastern seaboard, and its wetlands, including Chesapeake Bay and the estuary of the St. Lawrence River, became well known during the 16th century. By the 17th century Europeans had reached the wetlands of the Mississippi valley, led by French Jesuit missionaries, pioneer settlers, and trappers. To the north, in Canada, the fur trade was booming and led to the exploration of the western forests and wetlands and also north to the Hudson Bay region. One inspiration for westward exploration was the hope of finding a water route to the Pacific Ocean, but westward-running rivers became deflected north by the Rocky Mountains, leading to the Great Slave Lake. One of the early explorers was the Scotsman Alexander Mackenzie (1764–1820). In 1798 he set off on an expedition to find a route that would lead to the Pacific, and he discovered a river leading out of the Great Slave Lake that seemed certain to lead him to his objective. But this river, which he named the "River of Disappointment," also took him farther north, through rapids and deep ravines, eventually reaching the Arctic Ocean. The river later became known as the Mackenzie River and the lands around its mouth as the Mackenzie Delta. Although this river gave access to the wetlands of the High Arctic, it did not provide a route to the Pacific Ocean because the Arctic Ocean was frozen for much of the year. We now know that such a route does not exist.

The wetlands of the southern states of North America were steadily charted by the continued exploration of naturalists and settlers. James John Audubon (1785–1851) is one of the most important early explorers. He described the biodiversity of many of the southern swamplands. The swamps of what is now Florida were well known to the Spanish discoverers of the 16th century. Spain, in fact, claimed sovereignty over the region until the early 19th century. In the 18th century persecution displaced many Native American tribes in and around Florida, pushing some as far as the swamps of the Everglades. These people came into conflict with the American authorities by sheltering and befriending runaway slaves. General Andrew Jackson (1767–1845) led an army into the swamps in 1817 in what became known as the First Seminole War. When Jackson later became president of the United States (1829–37), he completed his war upon the Seminole people, forcing them out of the swamps along their "Trail of Tears" into relocation beyond the Mississippi River in 1842. Some militant groups of Seminoles remained in the swamps and continued the war, which is reckoned to have cost the lives of 1,500 American soldiers, apart from the uncounted Native American casualties. Even after the Third Seminole War of 1855 to 1858, many Seminole families held onto their rights as residents of America's greatest wetland, the Florida Everglades.

It is apparent that wetlands have played a significant part in the exploration of the planet. They have often proved of great value in supplying routes of transport into the interiors of continents. Rivers and lakes, even marshes and swamps, have often allowed explorers to gain access to regions that would have been difficult to reach by overland routes. Wetlands have sometimes been sought out by explorers for their own innate attraction and appeal, as in the search for the source of the Nile River, but they have also provided opportunities to reach many other natural regions of the world.

Wetlands in literature and art

Wetlands have contributed much to the exploration of the world, and they have also played an important role in the development of human culture. Water and wetlands are often important elements in novels, films, and paintings, and certain general principles seem to underlie the way in which wetlands are represented. Water is essential to all life, so it can become symbolic of living things and life-giving aspects of existence. On the other hand, water may be regarded as a sinister medium; we can drown in water, and it can be a source of disease and death. In art, water can represent both life and death, good and evil.

In general, however, moving water is associated with life and health, while stagnant water presents a threatening image. This is a very rational use of water as a symbol, because springs and fountains normally contain freshwater, free from contamination and disease, which is safe to drink. Fast-moving water does not sustain populations of bacteria or other microscopic life, some of which may be harmful if swallowed. Stagnant water, on the other hand, may be rich in bacteria and parasites. Contamination and the accumulation of harmful materials are much more likely to occur in water that does not move. Saline lakes are a good example of this because the salts that are brought in by streams become more concentrated as water evaporates and the residue remains. Thus, in literature and art moving waters often present an idyllic setting, while stagnant ones covey an air of threat and danger.

The Bible is rich in moving water imagery. Moses strikes a rock in the desert, and life-giving water flows. In the Book of Psalms a deer that is overheated by the chase relieves its thirst at a running stream. Jesus himself claims to be the source of living (literally moving) water that will satisfy those who drink. In classical writings oracles and fortune-tellers are often located at springs, thus conveying an image of purity and a satisfying supply for people's needs. There are exceptions to the general rule, however. False fountains in some stories lead people astray by promising goodness and actually supplying evil. In *The Fairie Queene* (1589) by Edmund Spenser, we read of a fountain that occasionally supplied evil waters that made the consumer grow faint and feeble. Interestingly, however, these times of deception were accompanied by the waters flowing more slowly. The Victorian writer William Morris was the author of a romantic novel with a strongly aquatic theme, *The Well at the World's End* (1896). It tells the story of a knight and a lady seeking the elusive well that would provide magical, strength-giving waters. When they are nearing their goal, however, they come across a false well containing putrid and poisonous water but having a superficial appearance of freshness and clarity. The lady warns her knight not to be deceived and to drink of it, for "when the wind eddies about it makes no ripple on the face of the pool, and doubtless it is heavy with venom." They continue on their journey to find the True Well with its revitalizing properties. Things are not always what they seem, and waters can deceive.

Just as moving waters are usually good, still waters are usually bad as represented in art. There are exceptions, of course, such as the still waters in Psalm 23, which are used to provide peace and tranquility in a hectic and stressful life, but more often than not, stagnant water is a source of evil. In classical mythology Hylas comes across a pool that is frequented by some very attractive nymphs, and he is entranced by their beauty. They entice him to join them in the pool, but when he does so, predictably, he is never seen again. This is another case of deceptive waters. Often, however, the stagnant waters in art display their evil nature without any hint of deception. The Pre-Raphaelite artist William Holman Hunt painted a picture of a goat stuck in the mud of the Dead Sea in Israel and entitled it *The Scapegoat* (1854). In an Old Testament ceremony, a priest transferred the sins of the entire people onto a goat, which was then driven into the wilderness to perish; the painting depicts the suffering beast approaching its doom in stagnant, saline waters. The art critic John Ruskin described the painting thus: "The air is stagnant and pestiferous, polluted by the decaying vegetation. Swarms of flies, fed on the carcasses, darken an atmosphere heavy at once with the poison of the marsh and the fever of the desert." The water in this painting does not flow, it pulsates in the heat, and it becomes a source of death rather than life.

Deep, still water inspires fears quite apart from that raised by the risk of disease transmission from slow-moving currents. The most obvious of these is the fear of drowning. In *Hamlet* (ca. 1600) William Shakespeare described the watery death of Ophelia in the following words: "But long it could not be/ till that her garments, heavy with their drink,/ pulled the poor wretch from her melodious lay/ to muddy death." Here is the awfulness of being pulled beneath the surface by one's sodden clothes. The situation becomes even more horrific if there is a rich supply of submerged aquatic vegetation that hampers one's attempts to escape the pull of the waters. In *The Lord of the Rings* (published 1954–55), J. R. R. Tolkien made good use of the horror of weed-choked pools in his description of the Dead Marshes encountered by the hobbits on their journey toward Mordor. "The only green was the scum of livid weed on the dark greasy surfaces of the sullen waters. Dead grasses and rotting reeds loomed up in the mists like ragged shadows of long-forgotten summers."

Such a morass of scum and weed raises another fear as well. It may harbor dangerous creatures, unseen beneath the murky surface but ready to attack. In the 1951 movie *The African Queen,* Humphrey Bogart wades through a swamp and emerges to find his body covered with blood-sucking leeches. The animals of the swamp do not need to be large to be a source of terror; but if they are large, then the terror is even greater. The 1954 film *The Creature from the Black Lagoon* featured a bipedal-gilled source of horror, discovered in the Amazon. Then there was the semivegetable, semihuman carnivorous plant that emerged from the mire in *The Swamp Thing* (1982). Deep within human psychology there is an innate fear of wetlands, particularly marshes and swamps where one's vision is restricted both above and below the water and where danger approaches without warning.

As represented by novels and movies, marshes and swamps are, as a rule, bad places. One notable exception is *Voyage to Venus* (1943; also called *Perelandra*) by C. S. Lewis.

This science fiction novel is set on the planet Venus, where the biblical fall of humankind into sin has not taken place and a couple like Adam and Eve still live in blissful innocence. They live, however, in a world of water, living on a floating mat of vegetation that undulates with the waves. It is a carpet of "vegetable broth of gurgling tubes and exploding bladders," and on this fibrous platform of instability, Lewis places paradise.

Bogs are almost invariably evil places in art and literature. The very word, with its brief harsh bark of sound, evokes a sinking feeling. If there is a prospect more dreadful than drowning in open water, it is the slow descent into the sucking peat of a bog pool. Bogs can be dangerous places, and any wetland ecologist who has inadvertently stepped into a soft spot and sunk up to the chest will appreciate that the habitat is bound to get bad press. Some of the great deaths in literature, especially of deserving villains, take place in bogs. In R. D. Blackmore's 1869 novel *Lorna Doone,* for example, the wicked Carver Doone ends his days gradually sinking in the mire and finally disappearing in a satisfying belch of marsh gas. In fact, at the site where he meets his literary doom, the blanket bogs of Exmoor in southern England, it would be difficult to find a patch of bog where one could sink up to the knees, but poetic license must operate and Carver Doone must die in the mire. Nearby Dartmoor is the setting for Arthur Conan Doyle's *The Hound of the Baskervilles* (1902), a classic of wetland horror stories. As Sherlock Holmes and Dr. Watson tramped over the Great Grimpen Mire in pursuit of the murderous Hound, "rank reeds and lush, slimy water plants sent an odor of decay and a heavy miasmatic vapor into [their] faces." One false step and they would sink thigh-deep into the peat only to find that "it was as if some malignant hand was tugging us down into those obscene depths." This is not the language of a vacation advertisement.

Wetlands, then, on the whole, have a rather poor image in art and literature. So many of them are represented as places where progress on one's journey is hindered rather than assisted. It is most unfortunate, although understandable given their physical characteristics, that wetlands have been used in this way by writers and artists. Their works have left humankind with a rather negative image of the wetland environment. Or perhaps it works the other way round and people's basic fear of wetlands has led artists and authors to use them in this way. However this situation has come about, it has led to prejudice against wetlands in human history. It is important, therefore, to consider just how valuable wetlands are.

Conclusions

Wetlands have played an important role in the history of human beings. In prehistoric times they were sometimes a barrier to human movements, but more often they have provided a means of travel as well as a source of food. Many early human settlements were close to wetlands, and the preservative properties of their sediments have often prevented the decay of remains of wooden structures and even human bodies, which serve as a source of information for modern archaeologists.

Many people around the world still live in wetland regions and exploit their rich resource to maintain their way of life. But wet regions provide a habitat for some organisms, such as mosquitoes and snails, that can carry dangerous parasites and can be the source of extremely harmful diseases, including malaria and schistosomiasis. Health efforts need to focus on breaking the chain of infection without destroying the wetland habitats.

Some of the greatest stories of intrepid exploration and adventure are associated with the discovery of wetlands and journeys through wetland habitats in order to penetrate into the interiors of continents. The rivers Nile, Congo, and Amazon have presented some of the greatest challenges that humans have had to face, and the stories of their exploration continue to inspire people even today.

Despite all that wetlands have given to humanity in these various ways, they are often used in art and literature to convey threatening and uncomfortable images. This may have emerged from a deeply implanted but misplaced fear of wetlands, a fear that people need to overcome.

CHAPTER 6

USES OF WETLANDS

The rich biodiversity and visual beauty of wetlands are such that people should value these regions for their own sake, but sadly this is not always so. Before people place a value on any object, they want to know "What use is it?" As it happens, it is not difficult to demonstrate the great value of wetlands to humanity. Wetlands act as reservoirs for precious water and absorb excess water that could otherwise result in damaging floods. They purify the water that passes through them and absorb some of the carbon dioxide that people are constantly pumping into the atmosphere. But human demands on wetlands have exceeded even these important services. Many of the world's wetlands have been exploited in a manner that is not sustainable. Peat has been extracted from many of the great bogs of the world, and large areas of wetland have been drained for agriculture and forestry. Wetlands are useful, but they are also misused.

Water conservation and flood control

Freshwater is a precious resource. As noted earlier, almost all of the water in the world is saline, and of the Earth's freshwater resources most are locked up in the ice sheets and glaciers of the polar and mountain regions (see "The water cycle," pages 1–3). Almost all of the nonmarine animals and plants of the world are dependent on the small amount of freshwater that remains, and that includes human beings. Some scientists believe that the supply of freshwater may ultimately limit how many people can live on our planet. The average American citizen uses 381 gallons (1,442 L) of water each day. The average resident of the European Union uses 150 gallons (566 L). Both of these regions are relatively rich in freshwater by global standards, but other areas of the world have to be much more careful in their use of water. At present about a third of the world's population lives under conditions of water scarcity. Climate change in the form of global warming over the next 100 years or so is calculated to bring an increase in global average precipitation, but this will not be evenly distributed. Many of the regions that currently experience adequate rainfall will be brought into conditions of regular drought.

All the freshwater that falls as precipitation will either move back into the atmosphere through evaporation and transpiration or will flow through rivers back to the oceans. Wetlands are reservoirs where the movement is temporarily slowed, and the water resides for a while on its journey. Any such delay in the movement toward the oceans should be welcome to people. The amount of water stored in a wetland varies with supply, decreasing in times of drought and increasing in times of plentiful rain. This stored water is valuable to human populations because it increases the likelihood of water being always available, even if its total volume is lower in the drought conditions. The presence of a wetland also reduces the danger of flooding during times of excessive rainfall. Taming the flood is one of the most valuable features of wetlands from a human point of view.

A flood is not always a harmful event. When a river overflows its banks and spreads over the surrounding land—the floodplain—the floodwater carries suspended sediments that have been eroded from higher in the catchment, and these add fresh materials to the soils they cover. In ancient Egypt the annual flooding of the Nile, caused by monsoon rains in the mountains of Ethiopia, was greeted as a sign of blessing from the gods. The spreading waters over the Nile floodplain fertilized and revitalized the soils on which Egyptian agriculture depended. Some farmers with land on floodplains have continued to make use of inundations, creating ditches to encourage the movement of water over grasslands in the early spring following snow melt. The water meadows created in this way receive the fertilizing effect of the floodwaters, and the moving waters also warm their soils, helping them to recover from the frosts of winter.

However, floods can also cause damage to human property, and this has led to the introduction of flood control measures in many regions of the world where dense human populations live on floodplains. In the Ganges Delta of Bangladesh, floods caused by waters draining all the way from the snows of the Himalaya Mountains frequently cause great suffering and loss of human life. In the Mississippi Delta of Louisiana, flooding has also been the cause of human fatalities and extensive damage to property. The control of floods has become an important concern for people in such areas. But water is a difficult medium to control, and bringing it into line in one area often results in additional problems downstream. In the case of the Mississippi, the construction of canals to improve transport has concentrated the water movements through the delta into certain channels, and in times of flood these are under strain. Instead of being able to move out over a floodplain, the confined water moves more rapidly along the routes that have been constructed by people. This places great pressure on the banks of the channels, and an unexpected breach can result in calamity, as with New Orleans in 2005. The canals also mean that sediments carried by the waters are no longer allowed to settle, but are carried out into the Gulf of Mexico, while saline waters can penetrate higher into the wetlands of the delta. Both of these processes have an adverse impact on the fishing industry of the region.

In Egypt the construction of the Aswān High Dam in the south of the country has ensured that the regular floods of the Nile are under control. This means that the cities built on the floodplain in the north of Egypt, such as Cairo, are now protected from rising water, but on the downside, the surrounding agricultural lands are denied the fertilizing effect of the spreading Nile waters. The sediment that would once have been carried down into the Nile Valley is now deposited behind the dam at Aswān, which means that the great reservoir that has been created behind the dam is rapidly becoming shallower. It is true that the waters of the Nile are now under tighter control and can be released for irrigation and other purposes exactly when they are needed, but the storage of very large volumes of water in one of the hottest and driest places on Earth does have some disadvantages. Evaporation is very high, and much of the stored water is lost in this way before it ever reaches Lower Egypt.

Higher up the Nile River are the great Sudd swamps and marshes of southern Sudan. This wetland covers 4,250 square miles (11,000 sq km) in which the waters of the Nile spread out over the desert landscape. The problem for the local population here is not the flooding risk but the difficulties of navigation through the papyrus marshes that are forever changing. The Sudd wetland presented one of the greatest problems for early explorers in their journeys up the Nile (see "Exploration of the wetlands," pages 139–148). In the 1970s a plan was devised to build a massive canal, the Jonglei Canal. Measuring 200 miles (350 km) long, the canal would simplify navigation by providing a direct route through the marshes for shipping. Construction began in 1978 but has never been completed, mainly because of engineering difficulties and the political instability of the region, but many wetland ecologists have been concerned about its effect on the movement of water through the Sudd. If completed, the dam would affect both the wildlife of the region and the local populations who rely on the marshes for fishing and pastoral activities.

Wetlands provide a natural system for flood control, but humans are often not content to accept their role in water management. The soils of floodplains are rich, so people attempt to recover them for agriculture. Historically, rivers have supplied one of the most useful means of transport, so most of the major cities of the world are situated either along coasts or in the floodplains of large rivers. Civilization, therefore, demands precisely the regions where wetlands have developed in the past. Even today crops need water for irrigation, and where this is not available through natural geography, people sometimes divert the courses of rivers. In China the Yangtze River has been diverted to irrigate new areas. In South America dams are being constructed within the Amazon basin to supply water for agricultural projects, and in the Pantanal region, which is one of the most important wetlands on that continent, plans to divert and extract water are a constant threat to the natural ecosystem. The Ob River of Russia is currently the subject of considerable debate; its waters could be redirected northward into the Arctic Ocean, supplying lands with irrigation water on its way. Environmental scientists are concerned, however, about the possible effect this would have on global hydrology and meteorology, perhaps inducing climatic changes in the Arctic.

Increasing human competition with wetlands for the limited water resources of the world is why wetland conservation is one of the most pressing conservation issues of our time.

Wetlands as a food source

Harvesting the products of wetlands provides a substantial source of income to people in many parts of the world, and the economic importance of wetlands, especially at a local level, needs to be taken into account when considering how they should be managed. Some of the products of wetlands can be managed and harvested in a sustainable fashion, including fish and reeds for thatching roofs. But, as in the case of all ecosystem exploitation, the products must not be removed faster than they can be regenerated.

Wild mammals that graze the wetlands are hunted as a source of protein in many parts of the world. Both the lechwe antelope of the Okavango Delta in Africa and the capybara of the Amazon wetlands in South America are hunted for their meat, and both are an important component of local diets. The caribou of the northern mires have long been hunted by Native Americans and have been brought into a state of semidomestication by the Sami (Lapp) peoples of Finland. Wetlands also provide a sustainable grazing resource for domesticated animals. About 800,000 cattle graze on the Sudd marshes of the southern Sudan, and the coastal wetlands of the Niger River delta in West Africa may support as many as 3 million cattle, sheep, and goats. In Southern Asia the water buffalo is an ideal domestic grazer for wetland areas because it is at home wading in deep water as it grazes. There is still much opportunity to bring other wetland-grazing animals, such as the lechwe and the capybara, into domestication so that this type of ecosystem can be used more effectively for human support without the need for drainage and conversion to conventional pasture land.

Wildfowl have long been harvested by hunters of the wetlands. Before the invention of gunpowder, fowlers would use nets to trap their prey, and some of the illustrations on the walls of ancient Egyptian tombs show that this method of exploiting wetlands for food dates back several thousand years. More sophisticated hunting techniques, particularly the use of firearms, have given hunters the capacity to harvest birds more effectively. But the success of hunting methods also demands that hunters control the extent of the harvest. Many wildfowl, especially in temperate regions, are migratory, and it is particularly important that the numbers of these birds are carefully monitored because overexploitation can easily take place in mobile populations. The ducks and geese especially need to be protected during their breeding season, and wetlands where breeding is abundant, such as the prairie pothole wetlands of North America (see photo), are particularly important in maintaining wildfowl populations.

Fisheries in wetlands are extremely important around the world. For instance, fish form a major part of the diet of the

Sunset over the prairie pothole wetlands of South Dakota. The prairie potholes are sometimes called the "Duck Factory" because they are the breeding grounds of many of the duck species hunted during the fall and winter. (Courtesy of Jim Brandenburg/ Minden Pictures)

Ugandan people living around the northern and western fringes of Lake Victoria. Fishing from dugout canoes and simple wooden boats, the fishermen are wary of the hippopotamus, which can be very aggressive and dangerous in the shallow wetlands. In the Mekong Delta of Southeast Asia the Grand Lac is said to be one of the most productive freshwater fisheries in the world, and some of the rivers of the region produce 50 to 80 pounds of fish per acre (60 to 90 kg per ha). In some coastal wetlands the harvest of crustaceans, such as shrimps and crabs, can be even more successful than that of fish. This is true of Jamaica and Taiwan. Farming fish and crustaceans in enclosures within the wetlands is proving an increasingly popular option. In Louisiana, for example, crawfish (or crayfish) are farmed in this way. The people of Bangladesh who live around the coastal mangrove wetlands keep bees that gather nectar and pollen from the wetland plants and provide a thriving honey industry.

Wetlands and water treatment

Wetland plants obtain their mineral elements directly from the water that moves past their roots. They need relatively large quantities of nitrates, phosphates, potassium, calcium, and magnesium, together with smaller amounts of sulfur, chlorine, iron, manganese, and various other trace elements. Consequently, water that has passed through a wetland, such as a marsh that contains an abundance of productive vegetation, will have lost a significant proportion of its dissolved substances to the growing plants. This is an important process considering that many of the materials that people deposit in water are actually plant nutrients. The process of eutrophication (see the sidebar on page 49) consists of the nutrient enrichment of waters as a result of such activities as sewage disposal, agricultural fertilizer runoff, and domestic wastewater. This enrichment is damaging to the natural aquatic ecosystems and can have a direct effect on human health. Excessive nitrates in drinking water can lead to the production of toxins in the stomach that may subsequently cause cancers, so the removal of these elements from water is an important part of water treatment.

The possibility of using wetlands as a means of cleaning water has been examined in some detail in Kenya, East Africa. Lake Naivasha in Kenya has become polluted by excessive sewage and fertilizer input, but the papyrus marshes around the mouths of incoming streams and rivers take up much of the plant nutrient load. Papyrus grows along the lakeshore but also forms floating rafts of vegetation. Sometimes these rafts break all connection with the fringing marsh and float out into the lake, but usually they retain some contact with the banks and stay anchored near the lake's edge. The emergent plants grow rapidly, and they derive their nutrients from the water that percolates through and beneath the mat of vegetation. In an experiment to check how much of the nutrient pollution had been removed from the water entering the lake, ecologists compared the chemistry of water emerging from the papyrus marsh with that entering the ecosystem. In the case of manganese, 94 percent had been removed; for iron it was 86 percent, sulfur 58 percent, and phosphorus 57 percent. The removal of nitrates, one of the major pollutants, proved difficult to determine because the marsh contained blue-green bacteria. These microbes fix nitrogen, so establishing a complete budget for nitrogen is difficult when they are present. Given the behavior of other plant nutrients, however, it is reasonable to suppose that nitrates were also removed by the papyrus.

Papyrus does not grow in the temperate climate of North America, but the common reed (*Phragmites australis*) does, and it behaves in a similar way. It is also a fast-growing species that demands considerable quantities of nutrients from the water that flows past its roots, so it can be used for water cleansing. Experimental studies using wetlands for water purification are very promising, particularly in situations where the establishment of more sophisticated systems is not possible. For example, reed beds can be used on roadsides where they can trap and treat contaminated water before it enters streams and rivers.

Wetlands as carbon sinks

All ecosystems that contain green plants take carbon out of the atmosphere. Plants remove carbon dioxide gas, and from these simple inorganic molecules they construct the complicated organic materials that form the basis of living things. Carbon compounds can be used for construction, but they can also be used for energy storage. Sugar, for example, is an energy storage compound in such plants as sugarcane, onion, and the wetland cattails. When energy is needed, as when the plant needs to extract a nitrate ion from the surrounding water, sugar is respired and carbon dioxide released into the atmosphere (or the water). As an ecosystem functions (see "What is an ecosystem?" pages 68–71), carbon is constantly removed from the atmosphere and then replaced. If the ecosystem is growing in its biomass, as when it is in the course of succession (see "Changing wetlands," pages 37–41), then it takes in more carbon than it gives out; it acts as a sink for atmospheric carbon. But when it is in a state of equilibrium and there is no more biomass growth, the carbon taken in is equal to the carbon given out; it is carbon-neutral.

Peat lands are extremely unusual ecosystems in that they store some dead organic matter in the soil beneath them, gradually building up a reserve of carbon. Thus an actively growing peat land acts as a sink for carbon as long as its peat mass keeps growing, which often means for thousands of years. Over the past 150 years we have seen the concentration of carbon dioxide in the atmosphere steadily rising, caused mainly by human activity in the form of burning fossil fuels and clearing extensive areas of forest. This has been accompanied by a similar rise in global temperature. Most climatologists now agree that the rise in carbon dioxide is a significant cause of the temperature rise because it traps heat energy being radiated by the Earth and retains it in the atmosphere or radiates it back to the ground. An atmosphere rich in carbon dioxide acts like a greenhouse, letting light in but retaining heat. Climate change will do much harm to wetlands and many other ecosystems, so it would be sensible to try to avoid this accumulation of carbon dioxide in the atmosphere. The question here is whether the peat lands can store carbon fast enough to help stem the tide of rising atmospheric carbon.

Most carbon storage is found in the temperate bogs of the Northern Hemisphere, because this is where decomposition is particularly slow and peat accumulates fastest. There are about 1.4 million square miles (3.5 million sq km) of these peat lands and they have an average peat-formation rate of 0.07 ounces per square foot (21 g per sq m) each year. This amounts to a total storage of carbon by peat lands of about 70 million tons each year. This may seem a very large quantity, but it is only a little more than 1 percent of the quantity of carbon people are injecting into the atmosphere by consuming fossil fuels. It would be easy to dismiss this as just a drop in the wetland, but every little counts in the effort to cut back on atmospheric carbon.

If the climate continues to become warmer, then the peat lands may no longer act as a sink for carbon. Warmer, drier conditions will result in faster decomposition, so less organic material will be stored as peat. Indeed, if the peat lands become significantly drier, then some of the stored peat may begin to oxidize; this would convert the wetlands from a carbon sink into a carbon source, and they would add to the abundance of carbon dioxide in the atmosphere. Under warmer conditions wetlands may also produce more methane gas, which is an incomplete oxidation product of organic matter. Methane is even more powerful than carbon dioxide as a greenhouse gas, so methane generation would make matters even worse. Much depends on precisely what course future global climate change takes. At present, it is likely that the high latitudes that are rich in peat lands may become warmer faster than the lower latitudes, so the future of the peat lands is not bright.

Wetlands and recreation

Recreation means to occupy oneself pleasurably, and wetlands offer many opportunities to do this. The word *recreation* (literally re-creation) involves an element of refreshment and renewal, and everyone needs to indulge in this. Recreation that involves interaction with the natural environment is one of two possible types. One is appreciative, in which a person is content to observe and study the environment, while the other is consumptive, which means that the person is taking something out of the environment. Walking, painting, boating, photographing, and watching wildlife are all appreciative activities. A habitat can sustain such activities as long as the disturbance that they entail does not become excessive, leading to the abandonment of the location by the wild creatures that are the object of the observations. Consumptive recreation includes hunting and fishing, where trophies are collected from the habitat, but it can also include thrill-seeking activities, pursuits that usually involve the pitting one's skills against nature at the expense of its tranquility. Activities such as speedboat racing, white-water rafting, and rock climbing can be included here.

A habitat can generally sustain less consumptive recreation than appreciative recreation, and the two types of activity do not generally mix well. Wetlands attract both types of recreation. Open-water environments are attractive to boating enthusiasts, for example, but their boats are generally a source of disturbance to bird life, removing the object of bird-watchers' interest. When wetlands of this type are to be used for recreation, it is often necessary to reserve certain areas for particular activities. For example, a lake may have one area designated for water-skiing, another for sailing, a third for angling, and a fourth area that can be protected from these consumptive activities and kept as a nature reserve. The four recreational activities listed here are in descending order of disturbance, and if they are arranged in this way, then a series of steps is created for wildlife protection. Where there are speedboats there will be few ducks. Some ducks, on the other hand, may be content to share the water with sailboats. Angling involves even less disturbance to the water birds and can be accommodated on the edges of a nature reserve area.

We may not think of bogs as a source of recreational activity, but in eastern Europe they are greatly appreciated by people who gather fungi and berries for consumption. Cranberries and blueberries grow on bogs, as do a variety of other species. This is a consumptive form of recreation, but it need not involve much damage if the density of gatherers is low. On the other hand, the effect of a single footprint on the surface of a sphagnum bog is quite considerable and it takes a long while to heal. In a study of the recovery of a footprint left on a Welsh bog, scientists discovered that even after two years the impression was still apparent, and it had involved a change in the plant species present. Bogs are therefore very sensitive to human recreational pressure. Where such sites are used for appreciative recreation by students of ecology or natural history, it is best to construct walkways that can bear the weight of visitors and confine them to specific paths, thus avoiding general trampling and damage to the vegetation.

Many of the world's wetland sites that are now reserved for appreciative recreation were once managed for exploitation. Indeed, many wetlands have escaped drainage and destruction simply because they were habitats in which hunting and fishing were successful. In India one of the most prolific wetlands on Earth is the Keoladeo Ghana National Park, near Bharatpur and not far from Agra and the Taj Mahal. In the late 19th century the Maharaja of Bharatpur visited Britain and was impressed by the pheasant and grouse-shooting recreation that he observed. He decided to use his wetland areas in the same way, so they became a site of recreational slaughter. He once managed to kill 4,273 birds in one day, and the fact that bird life still continued in the area illustrates how very rich in wildlife these wetlands were. The region is used by many migrating waterfowl, and large flocks of birds that breed in northern Asia spend the winter there. On the positive side, the Maharaja began to manage the site by building dams and causeways that would maintain high water levels throughout the year. Although he took a heavy harvest of birds, he also protected the wetlands and conserved the habitats that were needed to keep attracting more birds to the region. The site is now protected, and its survival and present use for appreciative recreation is largely due to its use as a source of consumptive recreation in the past.

This is not true of all wetland reserves, however. In the case of the Kakadu National Park in northern Australia, the site was maintained in a state of undisturbed tranquility by the native Aborigine people, who regarded the site as one of special spiritual significance. They took a harvest of fish and geese from the site, but it was not until commercial fisheries moved in that the stocks began to decline. Recently, the rise in "ecotourism" has brought new pressures upon this fragile region. The idea of ecotourism is that it is essentially appreciative rather than consumptive, and it aims at reducing to a minimum the environmental effect of the activities conducted. But all tourism is consumptive to some extent, requiring water, food, accommodation, and waste disposal, all of which place strains on the natural environment. In addition, there is the effect of large parties of visitors on the wildlife and the local human populations and their native cultures. Wetlands are particularly sensitive to such effects, being easily polluted and easily damaged and disturbed by visitors. The development of tourism, even of the appreciative variety, must therefore proceed with caution.

Peat exploitation

Many wetland types, especially the bogs of the temperate regions, are distinctive in their accumulation of organic sediments derived from the dead remains of the plants that have grown on the site. This growing peat deposit is a store of energy that microbes have failed to tap in their decomposition (see "Decomposition," pages 79–82). Human occupants of the boggy regions of the world have exploited this energy resource since prehistoric time, cutting and drying the peat, then burning it to release the energy as heat. While population densities were low, the environmental impact of local peat cutting was not serious, but growing populations and the loss of woodland as a source of combustible material led to increasing pressures on the bogs. In eastern Britain during medieval times, for example, peat was harvested so efficiently by the monks who owned the land that the holes left by the mining are still present today. They have now become flooded with water and have begun their succession over again, while providing a new source of recreation activity and nature conservation.

Commercial exploitation on a much bigger scale became possible with the industrial revolution and the development of machinery to drain the peat lands and cut the peat from the ground. Large areas of bog land in southern Canada, northern Europe, and Russia are now being harvested for their peat. In Ireland and Russia some of this peat is harvested for energy production on an industrial scale in power stations. But peat has other uses that have exerted even greater pressures on the diminishing resources of the bogs. Peat has some remarkable physical and chemical properties. It is able to absorb prodigious amounts of water; a saturated sample of sphagnum peat may consist of 95 percent water (see "Plants of the wetlands," pages 98–105). The organic material in peat also has the property of cation exchange, meaning that it can hold on its surface many of the nutrient elements in the soil or the water. These two features have resulted in the expanding use of peat in horticulture. Garden soil is improved by the addition of peat both because of its water-holding properties and its ability to bind with soil nutrients. Most garden plants benefit from the addition of peat to a soil, so it is not surprising that demand for peat has grown and the number of undisturbed bogs in the world has rapidly declined. Ireland was once regarded as a country rich in bogs, but there are now very few left in an undisturbed state. The United States, Canada, Germany, Finland, Estonia,

Peat harvesting in North Germany. Peat is mined for its energy content and also for horticulture because it is a valuable soil conditioner. But it is a nonrenewable resource, and wetlands devastated in this way can never recover their former condition. (Courtesy of Peter D. Moore)

and Russia are all moving along similar tracks, and bogs are under great threat.

Wetland drainage for agriculture and forestry

It is very apparent that wetlands are extremely useful ecosystems. The problem is that people have not always recognized their value; rather they have focused on the problems that an excess of water causes for agricultural production. As explained in chapter 4, plants generally have trouble coping with soil waterlogging because their roots are unable to obtain the oxygen they need to respire. This is particularly true of most crop plants, with the exception of rice, which is well adapted to wetland habitats. In most temperate areas wetlands were regarded as agricultural wastelands, and the only way of changing that idea was to lower the water table by drainage.

In 1919 the United States Department of Agriculture issued a map documenting wetlands "in need of drainage." It showed the East Coast from New Jersey down to, and including most of, Florida; the coastal regions of the entire Gulf of Mexico; the Mississippi Valley; and much of the Great Lakes region. By 1980 many of these areas had indeed been extensively drained for agriculture. Once drained, the peaty soils proved productive and fertile. In the last 100 years the United States has continued the practice of wetland drainage that has occupied humanity ever since the advent of plant domestication. In ancient Mesopotamia, Egypt, and Europe the drainage of wetlands was carried out wherever possible. In the lands surrounding the North Sea in northern Europe, the demand for agricultural land was so intense that coastal wetlands were reclaimed from the sea, drained, and gradually cultivated as their soils became less saline. In the 17th century Holland was reclaiming 4,000 acres (1,600 ha) of salt marshes and mudflats from the sea each year.

Removal of water from low-lying land presents some serious engineering problems. While the land to be drained lies above the level of the rivers and the sea, drainage can take place by gravity, but when an area of peat is drained the level of the soil itself falls as the water is removed. It may reach a point where the soil level is below sea level, or at least below the water level in the rivers. The water then needs to be pumped against the force of gravity in order to remove it from the land surface. In Holland this was initially achieved by pumps operated by windmills, but in 1787 the first steam engine pump was installed, and it was as effective at water removal as about 20 wind pumps. Wetland drainage and land reclamation received a considerable boost from this new technology.

In the United States most drainage projects date from the late 19th and early 20th centuries. Tile drains were introduced in 1870. These are tubes that are inserted in the soil and allow water to move more freely under the influence of gravity. The wet regions of the prairies became the focus of tile drainage, and by 1870 there were more than 1,000 tile factories operating in the prairie states. The consequences were enhanced productivity and a steep rise in land value. In the 40 years from 1870 to 1910, land prices in the prairie regions increased by a factor of five. Another effect was the reduction in malaria cases, because the loss of wetlands reduced the mosquito population of the region. In 1870 the annual malaria death rate was 30 per 100,000 of population, but this had fallen to 10 per 100,000 by 1890. The cost, however, was the loss of a biodiverse habitat.

In Florida more than 50,000 acres (20,000 ha) of wetland were drained to the north of Lake Okeechobee in the years between 1845 and 1865 and were planted with sugarcane and rice. Drainage to the south of the lake began in the 20th century with the construction of canals from Lake Okeechobee to Miami. Then came devastating hurricanes in 1927 and 1928 that left 2,500 people dead, mainly as a result of drowning in the floods, and this led to more concerted efforts to drain the wetlands. The swamps and marshes to the south were given the protected status of a National Park, but water extraction to the north starved the National Park of its water supply, leading to falling water levels in the Everglades. As the Atlantic coast region has developed, more water has been needed to support the growing population, so now only about half of the original wetland survives, and only one-fifth lies within the protection of the Everglades National Park. Whether water is taken for human use, or whether it is simply removed to enable crops to grow more effectively, the outcome is the same: Wetlands suffer.

Conclusions

Wetlands serve many human uses, quite apart from their value as a source of biological richness. They act as reservoirs for the Earth's precious, and very limited, supply of freshwater, providing a reliable supply of water even when conditions are dry. When wetlands act as storage reserves of water, they are also serving the function of flood control, because a sudden influx of water is retained to some extent within the wetland, thus reducing the effect of the flood downstream.

Wetlands also supply food in the form of fish, birds, and mammals to many of the peoples of the world, especially in developing countries. In this way they reduce the need for imported foodstuffs and contribute to local economies.

When water passes through marshes and swamps, the productive vegetation removes many of the elements that are needed for plant growth. Some of these elements, such as nitrogen and phosphorus, can be regarded as pollutants in the water; they are fertilizers, but they result in excessive growth of algae and can cause serious imbalance in the aquatic ecology. The removal of these harmful elements by marshland vegetation is a means of cleaning water before it moves farther downstream.

Peat lands are a particularly valuable type of wetland because they lock up carbon from the atmosphere in their peat deposits and thus reduce, if only to a small extent, the harmful effects that result from human atmospheric pollution with carbon dioxide. Peat lands are an important element in the global cycling of carbon, and people need to keep them healthy and actively growing to ensure that they continue to operate in this way.

Wetlands are also of value as recreational areas. Some recreational activities are appreciative, involving simple observation without, if possible, damage to the object of study. Other activities are consumptive; they take things out of the environment, such as a harvest of fish or fowl, or they may remove the tranquility of the habitat through recreation that disturbs it. Conservation and recreation can be reconciled, but it requires careful management.

Unfortunately for wetlands, they create one product that has proved of industrial value to humans, namely peat. People extract this commodity for energy production or for soil improvement in fields and gardens. Peat is a nonrenewable resource, however, and its use destroys a habitat that has taken thousands of years to grow and cannot be replaced for countless generations.

Wetlands are often perceived as wastelands, and they have been reclaimed for agriculture and forestry throughout the history of farming. The land upon which wetlands grow is often of high productive value, so people have often sought to drain the wetlands to bring them into production for either food or timber.

All of these uses of wetlands can potentially threaten their survival.

CHAPTER 7

THE FUTURE OF WETLANDS

Wetlands are among the world's most sensitive habitats. They are delicately balanced with their environment and are affected by any change, however small, in the atmosphere, the water supply, or local land use. As explained in chapter 6, many wetlands occupy sites that can become very fertile agricultural land if drained, and the peat recovered from some wetlands is economically valuable. The outcome is that wetlands are extremely fragile and vulnerable habitats. Their fragility means that they are very easily damaged, possibly beyond repair, while their vulnerability means that they are under threat because of the alternative uses to which they can be put. As human populations expand, demands for land and food production increase, and so do the pressures placed on wetlands. Consequently, these valuable ecosystems will inevitably decline unless people actively conserve and manage them now.

Rates of wetland loss

In the developed nations of the world, such as the United States and many European countries, a large proportion of wetlands has already been lost, either to peat extraction or agricultural development. In America, wetlands continue to be converted to farmland at a rate of about 600,000 acres (250,000 ha) per year. Obviously, the farmer wishes to maximize the economic productivity of the land, and wetlands often provide no income. There are also tax incentives that encourage drainage, resulting in unproductive land (including wetlands) being brought into cultivation. Fortunately for the wetlands, there are also agencies operating that encourage the preservation and conservation of the more valuable wetlands. The U.S. Fish and Wildlife Service, acting on the

171

basis of the Wetlands Loan Act of 1961, is empowered to provide interest-free federal loans for the private acquisition of wetlands for conservation. Similarly, the Coastal Zone Management Act of 1972 empowers the Office of Coastal Management to provide funding for state wetland initiatives. Local wildlife and hunting interests also encourage the protection and even the rehabilitation of damaged wetlands, as is the case in many of the prairie pothole wetlands of the Midwest.

The conservation movement has been strong in the United States for well over 100 years. The American people in general have a respect for wilderness that is relatively rare in other parts of the world, and this has led to better preservation of wetland and many other habitats than might otherwise have been the case. The study of natural history as a hobby, particularly birding, is a major recreational growth industry, and this has resulted in the development of large and powerful conservation organizations and political lobbies. Even so, many great wetland areas in the United States have been lost and continue to be damaged. In Europe a similar rise in conservation interest in recent decades has come almost too late. High population density, combined with land reclamation schemes that date back many centuries, have left Europe with few wilderness areas to match the U.S. national parks. Political fragmentation has also denied Europe any unified conservation or agricultural policies. The development of the European Union of nations in recent years may help to establish international programs of wetland conservation, but at present the rate of land drainage and agricultural reclamation in just England and France exceeds that of the whole United States.

Many of the world's most important wetlands lie in the developing countries of the Tropics, and here the threat facing them is very great. In 1971 an international conference was held in the town of Ramsar, Iran, on the shores of the Caspian Sea. This international gathering served many purposes. It defined the word *wetland*, and it also selected certain sites around the world, so-called Ramsar Sites, which were considered to be of supreme international importance. Various nations signed the Ramsar Convention and pledged their support in the conservation of these special sites. Unfortunately, not all nations of the world felt able to commit themselves to this convention, among them many of the nations of South America. As a consequence, many very valuable South American wetlands are under particular threat, including those in the floodplain of the Orinoco River in Venezuela, which are being cleared and drained for cattle grazing. In southern Brazil the enormous flooded grasslands and forests of the Pantanal are also under great pressure for agricultural reclamation.

In the Niger River delta of West Africa the wetlands that have long supplied the needs of tribal peoples and their grazing animals are now under threat from the development of dams and flood-control schemes. Inevitably, the harnessing of floodwaters in this way will result in wetland loss, just as the Aswan Dam in Egypt has done as it controls the annual flood of the Nile River. Sometimes wetland drainage has been politically motivated, as in the drainage of the marshes of southern Iraq, where a major motive was the destruction of the way of life of the Marsh Arabs of the region. In the Far East the coastal swamps of Indonesia are in great danger as rapidly rising populations increase the demand for land and food supply.

Wetland losses worldwide are a cause for concern, but the Ramsar Convention has brought attention to the need for international cooperation in wetland conservation. Although the convention has no force in international law, it is a means of encouraging nations to gain prestige by leading the way in the conservation movement.

Wetland pollution

Wetlands are great collectors and accumulators: They collect energy and store it up as peat, and they collect eroded mineral fragments and build them up in their sediments. In the same way they also collect pollutants. Rheotrophic mires, which receive water draining from catchments, are particularly effective as collectors, picking up any chemicals that drain into the waters of the surrounding land. These may be fertilizers used in excess by farmers or foresters; elements released into drainage waters when changes in landscape management take place, such as the felling of forests or the plowing of grasslands; or pollutants deposited into streams and rivers by industrial plants, such as the mercury that was formerly used in the paper pulp industry to prevent fungal contamination of the manufactured paper. Mercury has affected lakes and coastal wetlands, and this toxic element has accumulated in wetland food webs and eventually reached human beings. Between 1953 and 1961 in the bay of Minamata, Japan, mercuric sulfate from an industrial plant polluted coastal wetlands, including mud-dwelling mollusks that accumulated the poison. Local fishers ate the mollusks and suffered mercury poisoning, which resulted in the death of 65 people before the cause was detected.

Aluminum is not so toxic as mercury, but it has become a problem in recent years because it can cause the death of fish. Aluminum is more soluble in acid waters, and the problem has arisen because the acidity of rain has greatly increased over the last 200 years, mainly as a consequence of industrial activities and the burning of fossil fuels. Coal emits sulfur and nitrogen oxides when it is burned, and these compounds dissolve in water to produce sulfuric and nitric acids. The resulting acid rain has made many wetland ecosystems more acidic, and this has affected invertebrate and fish populations. But the most serious effect has occurred in the northern countries of Canada, Sweden, Norway, and Finland, where tainted snow builds up during the winter and then melts in the spring. The sudden flush of acidic water dissolves aluminum out of the soil and carries it into the wetlands in a sudden surge. This acute exposure to acidity accompanied by aluminum toxicity is particularly damaging to aquatic life.

Pesticides also move into wetlands through the incoming streams, and these can build up both in sediments, where they are buried out of harm's way, and in the living creatures of the ecosystem. One of the worst of these was DDT, an insecticide that was widely used during and after World War II. It was considered harmless to people, but the tests that determined this were based on a few doses rather than on prolonged exposure. DDT was sprayed directly into many wetlands because it controlled the populations of mosquitoes and thus reduced human infection with malaria. Even outside the malaria zone, insect control using DDT became very popular, and it was sprayed on the wetlands surrounding Clear Lake in California. Local anglers, who had welcomed this move, soon found that fish were dying. This was followed by the deaths of fish-eating birds, such as grebes and herons. It was some time before people appreciated that DDT was the cause of the problem because the concentration of this pesticide in the water was very low, only 0.015 parts per million. But when analysts studied the fatty tissues of dead birds, they found concentrations of 1,600 parts per million. The compound evidently accumulated in the wetland food chain and reached fatally toxic levels in the predatory birds. The buildup of DDT was later found to be widespread among predators, and populations of bald eagles and peregrine falcons declined rapidly. A global ban of this seemingly promising pesticide was the only answer, and the subsequent recovery of the populations of many bird predators has confirmed that this compound had been the cause of their decline.

Although rheotrophic wetlands are the most sensitive to pollution because of their collecting properties, the ombrotrophic peat lands are not immune to pollution. Since they obtain their water entirely from precipitation, the only way that pollutants can reach them is from the atmosphere. The acid rain caused by fossil fuel burning falls upon the temperate bogs and does affect their pH. Because these bogs are already acid as a consequence of the chemical influence of the sphagnum bog mosses, the additional acidity brought by the rain does not seem to have any harmful effects. But the rain brings other problems. Ammonia and nitrates in the rain are much more serious for the bogs. Ombrotrophic mires are populated by organisms that exist at very low levels of mineral nutrients. Ammonia and nitrates fertilize such ecosystems, and when they enter these wetlands, the conditions improve for more competitive plant species, such as certain grasses, which can outcompete and eliminate the true bog species. Many of the bogs that lie downwind of industrial areas are showing signs of becoming eutrophic as a result of air pollution, and their vegetation is gradually changing.

Climate change and wetlands

Wetlands are sensitive to the climate because they are dependent on water supply. The rain-dependent ombrotrophic mires are more sensitive because they are directly affected by any slight change in rainfall, whereas the rheotrophic wetlands collect their water over a wide catchment and are therefore less sensitive. But even these rheotrophic wetlands may suffer if the climate becomes warmer and drier, especially if they exist in arid regions. The Coto Doñana wetlands of southern Spain, for example, lie in a very hot and dry region of the world. They are fed by a large river, but when the normal winter rains of the region failed for several consecutive years in the early 1980s, the landscape turned from marsh to desert.

A peat land that is directly dependent on rainfall will be able to keep its surface wet only while the amount of water received by precipitation is equal to or exceeds the amount of water lost by evaporation, transpiration, and surface

The marshes of the Coto Doñana wetlands in southern Spain occasionally suffer from drought when the water cover and the marsh vegetation are lost. Wildfowl and other animals suffer during these periods of climatic stress. (Courtesy of Peter D. Moore)

drainage. If precipitation decreases or becomes restricted to particular times of the year, or if the temperature rises, encouraging higher rates of evapotranspiration, the water supply at the bog surface will decrease. When water becomes scarcer, the upper layers of plant litter will decay more rapidly because air will penetrate better into the litter, encouraging the activities of the fungi and bacteria. This means that peat ceases to accumulate. Bog growth, then, is very sensitive to climate change.

In a cut face of peat, exposed, for example, when peat is being extracted from a site, past growth rates are apparent in the color of the different layers. A pale-colored peat indicates fast growth and poor decomposition, which is a response to wet and cool conditions. A dark peat, on the other hand, indicates slow growth and fast decomposition, which accompanies dry and warm conditions. A study of the different layers of peat can therefore provide evidence for past climatic conditions. This area of research is becoming increasingly important in the search for insight into the climatic fluctuations of the past.

Climatic records of the past 150 years show that the global climate has become warmer by about 3°F (1.5°C). Most scientists now agree that this change is at least partly due to the effects of human beings burning fossil fuels and clearing the world's forests, thus releasing extra quantities of the greenhouse gas carbon dioxide into the atmosphere. What is not known is whether the current rise may also be part of longer-term natural fluctuations. Whatever the contributing factors that have caused the current rise in world temperature, it is fairly safe to extrapolate from the present curve and predict that global conditions will continue to get warmer. Will this have an effect upon the wetlands?

That question raises another: Is climate change taking place at the same rate in all areas? The answer is no. The Northern Hemisphere is warming faster than the Southern Hemisphere, which is one reason why scientists think that humans are contributing to the problem, for industrial activity is far greater in the Northern Hemisphere. But even within the Northern Hemisphere, temperature rise is unequally distributed, with the fastest change taking place in the far north.

This means that the high-latitude bogs of the boreal and Arctic regions will be subject to the greatest rise in temperature, which is bad for the bogs. What is not yet clear from meteorological predictions is how the pattern of precipitation will be affected. Higher temperature could bring faster evaporation from the oceans and produce more rainfall, but where the rain will occur depends on changing patterns of airflow, so current models of climate leave many questions unanswered.

If the temperature of the northern wetlands does increase without any substantial increase in precipitation, then peat formation can be expected to slow down or cease altogether, which would mean that the peat lands were no longer acting as a sink for atmospheric carbon. Indeed, if the bogs become really dry, then they may become a source of carbon as the peat deposits begin to decompose. They could also emit methane, another greenhouse gas, into the atmosphere. There is a very real danger, in other words, that global warming may reverse the carbon-absorbing properties of the bogs and even turn them into a source of further warming in a kind of positive feedback effect.

A raised bog on the North Sea coast of Germany. The sea level is rising, and the bog is gradually being eroded and replaced by salt marsh. If global climate continues to become warmer, then sea levels will rise and place pressures upon coastal wetlands. (Courtesy of Peter D. Moore)

If the world's climate continues to become warmer, then one inevitable effect will be melting ice sheets and glaciers, leading to a rise in global sea level. The ocean waters themselves will also expand as they warm, enhancing the rise. If this takes place, then coastal wetlands will be at risk, and there are signs of this occurring in some locations. In northern Germany, for example, the coastal bogs are gradually being invaded by the advancing sea (see photo). The effect of a rising sea level will be even more serious for the mangrove swamps of the Tropics.

Wetland rehabilitation and conservation

Many of the world's wetlands have been badly damaged by drainage for forestry and agriculture and for peat extraction, but have they been destroyed beyond repair, or can ecologists still put some of them back together again? Many conservationists have become concerned with the possibilities of rehabilitating damaged wetlands and recovering lost habitats.

Some types of wetland are relatively easy to build. Flooding an area and maintaining a high water level results in rapid development of a wetland that can soon acquire characteristic flora and fauna. Many wetland plants and animals are remarkably efficient at moving around, either being washed downstream in the water flow or being carried by migrating birds, in mud on their feet or, in the case of seeds, passing through the bird's digestive system and being expelled in the next wetland visited. Emergent plants, such as cattails and reeds, rapidly establish themselves in shallow water, so it is not difficult to construct a marsh environment. Artificial marshes are often used for the initial treatment of waste and polluted water (see "Wetlands and water treatment," pages 159–160). The maintenance of high water levels, however, is important if a marsh is to be sustained, because the plants are sensitive to periods of drought. This is an important consideration if the water body is being used as a means of water storage and will be occasionally drawn upon for irrigation or other purposes, including hydroelectric power generation. The periodic drop in water levels associated with many artificial reservoirs means that their shores are not suitable for wetland development, and they rarely develop marshland habitats that can be sustained.

If the water level can be maintained, however, building a marsh is not too difficult a task. Keeping it as a marsh may be more demanding. As sediment accumulates and water becomes shallower, trees will invade and the process of succession will take place (see "Changing wetlands," pages 37–41). Soon the herbaceous marsh begins to turn into a forested swamp. This may be the desired result, but if instead the goal is to retain beds of reeds and cattails in which bitterns can breed, the process of tree invasion must be controlled. This can be achieved by eliminating trees by hand as they appear, which is labor-intensive and may therefore prove expensive; or the reed bed can be mowed in late summer or fall (when the water level is at its lowest), thus preventing trees from gaining a firm foothold in the ecosystem. In days when reed beds were managed for the production of thatch, regular mowing ensured that succession was halted and maintained at the required stage.

Other management techniques can be applied that are rather more extreme and catastrophic but may be cheaper to operate. Burning reed beds periodically can serve a similar function to mowing because it removes the excess biomass. The detonation of explosives in a reed bed is a very effective way of creating open water areas in which the process of invasion and colonization by emergent plants can start over again. This may not sound like good conservation, but it is a very effective way of creating and maintaining a habitat with different stages in the succession, together with all the associated species.

If no management is applied to a marsh wetland, then succession will proceed and reed beds will be replaced by swamp forests. This stage in wetland succession is quite a stable one and will persist for a long period of time. Most trees survive longer than humans, so effectively the wetland will remain in this condition indefinitely. Sphagnum-dominated raised bogs, on the other hand, are effectively impossible to create because they take too long. Conservationists can plan for tens of years, possibly even a hundred years into the future, but producing a program that will take a few thousand years is just not practicable. The raised bog, therefore, is effectively irreplaceable and can never be rebuilt once it has been destroyed.

Peat lands that have been damaged may still be restored, however, depending on how much peat has been removed and how far water tables have been lowered. If a peat land has been drained for forestry, the damage may only be a few feet deep. Blocking the drainage channels that have been constructed over the bog surface may be adequate as a means of raising the water table back to its former level. The natural plants of the area, including the bog mosses, may survive on the damaged surface, or they can be reintroduced quite easily because sphagnum grows readily from small fragments of stems and branches. One of the main problems is the invasion of trees such as birch. Birch fruits are small and easily carried by wind, so they rapidly invade bare peat surfaces and establish themselves. Removal is difficult because the saplings are often dense and abundant. Burning is not a good control method because it results in the fertilization of the peat land, and this encourages competitive species that will outcompete the bog mosses. Many cutover bogs have been rehabilitated by raising the water table and controlling tree invasion. The outcome is rarely as spectacular, as extensive, or as diverse as a pristine and undamaged bog, but it is often worth the effort to reestablish the distinctive flora and fauna of these ancient ecosystems.

Attitudes toward conservation have changed greatly over the past 50 years. At one time it was believed that nature was perfectly capable of looking after itself and that the best treatment for any habitat was simply to leave it alone. It has become increasingly evident that this is not so. Perhaps before humans had appeared on the planet and conducted their own global experiments in changing the face of the Earth, nature was indeed capable of dealing with catastrophe and healing any damage. People, however, have created a very new set of circumstances on this planet. We have so modified the world that any restoration requires further human involvement. For example, studies indicate that some habitats in the United States, including forests and chaparral, have long been influenced by fire. Lightning strikes and the activities of Native American people have ensured that fire has been a regular feature in their history. During the last century, efforts to reduce human pressures on the environment have often resulted in the prevention of fire, when fire was needed for the healthy continuance of the habitat. The results have been all too obvious in recent years, with the disastrous fires in Yellowstone National Park in 1989 and the severe fires in California in 2003. Regular and deliberate fire management could have reduced the effect of these catastrophes by preventing the buildup of inflammable materials to dangerous levels. The same rule applies to almost all Earth's biomes: People have the responsibility both to preserve and to manage the environment. Conservation, as we now understand the concept, involves more than just preservation; it requires deliberate and considered management to ensure that the balance in ecosystems is maintained.

We live in days when the influence of human beings is apparent even in the most remote wildernesses on Earth. Pesticides are present in the penguins of Antarctica and plastic bottles can be found floating in the middle of the Atlantic Ocean. Wetlands have been most severely affected because we have damaged them deliberately in land reclamation and accidentally by pollution. We can never fully recover the wetlands we have lost, but we can ensure that we retain representative examples of the wetlands that remain. Wetlands are reservoirs of biodiversity and are archives of past conditions; they have much to teach us if we are willing to learn.

Conclusions

Because wetlands are unproductive in agricultural terms, they have been perceived as wastelands and have been reclaimed by drainage throughout much of the developed world. The process is continuing right up to the present day. The developing nations are also eager to expand their agricultural production, so the wetland losses already recorded by the developed nations are being repeated in the Tropics.

The wetlands that remain are sensitive to many forms of environmental change. In particular, they accumulate many of the toxins that human activities liberate into the environment. Waterborne pollutants collect over watersheds and concentrate in the rheotrophic wetlands of the valleys. Here the toxin, whether a heavy metal, such as mercury, or a pesticide, such as DDT, may be stored in sediments or pass through the food webs and accumulate in the top predators. The predator may be human, in which case the toxicity has a direct impact upon people.

Climate change is likely to affect wetlands, especially the bogs of the northern regions, where temperature is expected to rise more rapidly than elsewhere. The likely outcome is the drying of bogs, the decomposition of peat, and an additional input of carbon to the atmosphere, making the problem of climatic warming even worse. Rising sea levels will also affect coastal wetlands.

Some wetlands can be created, especially those that occupy an early stage in succession, including shallow-water wetlands and marshes. If they are to continue in this state, however, they need active management in the form of harvesting or excavation to halt the progress of the succession to forested swamps. If space is available, then a range of wetland habitats can be maintained by creating a mosaic of different stages in succession. This results in the greatest possible diversity of species.

Conservation, therefore, involves more than just preservation, simply putting a fence around wetlands and keeping people out. Instead, we must become actively involved with their management to ensure that their great wealth of biodiversity is maintained. Such management, however, must be based on accurate knowledge of how wetlands work, and this knowledge can be gained only by intensive study of these remarkable ecosystems.

GLOSSARY

aapa mire   sloping fens found in the boreal regions of North America and Eurasia. A series of ridges (strings) and linear pools (flarks) run across the slope of the fen, giving these mires a distinctively striped appearance when seen from the air. In North America aapa mires are sometimes referred to as "string bogs," but the term *bog* is not strictly accurate because bogs are ombrotrophic (rain-fed) while aapa mires are rheotrophic (flow-fed)

acrotelm   the upper layers of peat at the surface of a mire that consist of uncompacted dead organic matter. Water moves with ease in the acrotelm; it has a high hydraulic conductivity. These layers are periodically aerated when the water table falls. Decomposition is therefore faster in the acrotelm than in the catotelm below

active layer   the upper soil layers in Arctic permafrost environments, which melt in the summer and freeze in the winter

aestivation   a period of dormancy that certain animals undergo to avoid the unfavorable conditions of summer drought (equivalent to hibernation in winter)

allochthonous   describing material that has originated away from the site in which it eventually settles, such as leaves carried into a lake; the opposite of autochthonous

allogenic   describing forces outside a particular ecosystem that may cause internal changes; for instance, rising sea level can influence water levels in freshwater wetlands farther inland and is therefore considered an allogenic factor

anaerobic   lacking oxygen (= anoxic)

anion   elements or groups of elements carrying a negative charge, such as NO_3^- or HPO_3^-

anoxic   lacking oxygen (= anaerobic)

autochthonous   describing material that has originated in the site where it is deposited, such as bog moss peat in a bog. The opposite of allochthonous

185

autogenic   forces within an ecosystem that bring about changes, for instance the growth of reeds in a marsh result in increased sediment deposition. *See also* FACILITATION

biochemical (or biological) oxygen demand   the amount of dissolved oxygen used up during the breakdown of organic pollutants in a water body. It is used as an index of organic pollution in water

biodiversity   the full range of living things found in an area, together with the variety of genetic constitutions within those species and the range of habitats available at the site

biomass   the quantity of living material within an ecosystem, including those parts of living organisms that are part of them but are strictly nonliving (such as wood, hair, teeth, claws) but excluding separate dead materials on the ground or in the soil (termed litter)

biosphere   those parts of the Earth and its atmosphere in which living things are able to exist

blanket mires   ombrotrophic (rain-fed) wetlands (true bogs) found in regions of high precipitation, mostly in cool temperate, oceanic regions, but also on some tropical mountains. Blanket peat deposits extend over valley floors, hilltop plateaus, and even over all but the steepest of hill slopes

blue-green bacteria (cyanobacteria)   microscopic, colonial, photosynthetic microbes, which are able to fix nitrogen; once wrongly called blue-green algae. They play important ecological roles in some wetlands as a consequence of their nitrogen-fixing ability, such as in rice paddies

bog   a wetland ecosystem in which the water supply is entirely from rainfall (ombrotrophic), including raised bogs, blanket bogs, and bog forest. Such wetlands are acidic and poor in nutrient elements. They accumulate a purely organic peat with very little mineral matter (derived solely from airborne dust), so are prized for horticulture

bog burst   a catastrophic and sudden erosion of peat masses resulting from their development on unstable slopes and absorption of excessive loads of rainwater

bog forests   acidic, ombrotrophic (rain-fed), domed tropical mires (true bogs) that accumulate deep peat deposits in some equatorial coastal regions, particularly in Southeast Asia. They are regarded as the closest modern equivalent to the Carboniferous coal-forming swamps

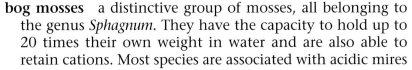

bog mosses a distinctive group of mosses, all belonging to the genus *Sphagnum.* They have the capacity to hold up to 20 times their own weight in water and are also able to retain cations. Most species are associated with acidic mires

boreal northern, usually referring to the northern temperate regions of North America and Eurasia, which are typically vegetated by evergreen coniferous forests and wetlands. Named after Boreas, the Greek god of the North Wind

calcareous rich in calcium carbonate (lime)

capillaries fine tubelike air spaces found in the structure of partially compacted peat or soil

carr in European usage, a forested rheotrophic (flow-fed) wetland; equivalent to the North American term *swamp*

catchment a region drained by a stream or river system (equivalent to the term *watershed*)

cation an element or group of elements with a positive charge, such as Na^+, NH_4^+, or Ca^{++}

cation exchange the substitution of one positively charged ion for another. Certain materials (such as peat and clay) have the capacity to attract and retain cations and to exchange them for hydrogen in the process of leaching

catotelm the deeper, compacted layers of peat, which are permanently waterlogged and anoxic and which have a very low hydraulic conductivity (they are virtually impermeable to water). Decomposition within the catotelm is very slow, in contrast to the acrotelm

charcoal incompletely burned pieces of organic (usually plant) material. These are virtually inert and hence become incorporated into lake sediments and peat deposits, where they provide useful indications of former fires. Fine charcoal particles may cause changes in the drainage properties of soils, blocking soil capillaries and leading to waterlogging and mire formation, as in the case of many valley mires and blanket mires

climate the average set of weather conditions over a long period in a region

climax the supposed final, equilibrium stage of an ecological succession. Many would question whether real stability in nature is ever achieved

coal ancient peats that have been physically and chemically altered as a consequence of long periods of compression, sometimes at high temperature, and can be used as fuel

community   an assemblage of different plant and animal species, all found living and interacting together. Although they may give the appearance of stability, communities are constantly changing as species respond in different ways to such environmental alterations as climate change

competition   an interaction between two individuals of the same or different species arising from the need of both for a particular resource that is in short supply. Competition usually results in harm to one or both competitors

coppicing   a management system applied to certain trees and shrubs in which the stems and branches are cut back to a low stump or "stool" only a few inches above ground level. Buds on the stool ensure that the plant regrows, producing new shoots for future harvests, and managers usually apply cutting in a cycle of between 10 and 20 years. The system of wood harvesting has been used for at least 5,000 years in Europe

cyanobacteria   *see* BLUE-GREEN BACTERIA

deciduous   describing a plant that loses all its leaves during an unfavorable season, which may be particularly cold or particularly dry

decomposition   the process by which organic matter is reduced in complexity as microbes use its energy content, usually by a process of oxidation. As living things respire the organic materials and produce carbon dioxide, other elements such as phosphorus and nitrogen return to the environment where they are available to living organisms once more. Decomposition is therefore an important aspect of the nutrient cycle

detritivore   an animal (usually invertebrate) that feeds upon dead organic matter

diatoms   a group of one-celled photosynthetic organisms that form an important part of the phytoplankton in wetland habitats. They construct cases (frustules) made of silica, which survive in lake sediments and indicate past conditions, such as the acidity of water bodies. They are thus useful in the study of environmental history

domed mire   *see* RAISED BOG

dune slack   a wet fen ecosystem found in a hollow between sand dunes. As a result of the calcium carbonate (lime) in broken mollusk shells within the sand, these slacks are often fed by lime-rich groundwater

eccentric bog a type of raised, rain-fed mire that develops on gentle slopes, forming pool systems that instead of being uniformly concentric in arrangement have their focus in the upper section of the mire while the pools assume a crescentic form downslope

ecosystem an ecological unit of study encompassing the living organisms together with the nonliving environment within a particular habitat

emergent aquatic plants wetland plants that are rooted in soil that lies underwater but have shoots projecting above the water surface

erosion the degradation and removal of materials from one location to another, often by means of water or wind

eutrophication an increase of fertility within a habitat, often resulting from pollution by nitrates or phosphate from runoff of these materials into water bodies from surrounding land. This increase in fertility results in enhanced plant (often algal) growth followed by death, decay, oxygen depletion, and anoxia. Very few animals can survive under anoxic conditions, so eutrophication often leads to low-diversity aquatic ecosystems

evaporation the conversion of a liquid to its gaseous phase. The term is often applied to the loss of water from terrestrial and aquatic surfaces

evapotranspiration a combination of evaporation from land and water surfaces and the loss of water vapor from plant leaves (transpiration)

evaporite a sediment rich in salts resulting from the evaporation of warm shallow lakes

evergreen a leaf or a plant that remains green and potentially able to photosynthesize through the year. Evergreen leaves do eventually fall but may last for several seasons before they do so

facilitation the process by which a plant species alters its local environment such that other plants can invade. For example, when a water lily grows in a lake, its leaf stalks slow the movement of water, causing suspended sediments to settle. The lake consequently becomes shallower, permitting other plant species to invade and eventually supplant the water lily. Facilitation is one of the forces that drives ecological succession

fen a wetland dominated by herbaceous plants, fed by the flow of groundwater (rheotrophic) and having its summer water table at or below the soil surface

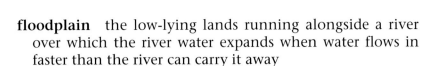

floodplain   the low-lying lands running alongside a river over which the river water expands when water flows in faster than the river can carry it away

food web   the complex interaction of animal feeding patterns in an ecosystem

fossil   ancient remains, usually the buried remnants of a once-living organism; the term can be applied to ancient buried soils or even the organic remains termed fossil fuels

fragility   an expression of the ease with which an organism or a habitat may be damaged. Fragile ecosystems, such as many wetlands, need careful conservation

frustule   the silica shell of a diatom. The frustule has two valves, which fit together like the overlapping base and lid of a box

fundamental niche   the potential of an organism to perform certain functions or to live in certain areas. Such potential is not always achieved because of competitive interactions with other organisms. *See also* REALIZED NICHE

greenhouse effect   the warming of the Earth's surface due to the interaction between radiation and Earth's atmosphere. Short-wave solar radiation passes through the atmosphere unchanged, but Earth's surface radiates it as long-wave radiation (heat). The atmosphere then absorbs the long-wave radiation because of the presence of greenhouse gases

greenhouse gas   an atmospheric gas that absorbs long-wave radiation and therefore contributes to the warming of the Earth's surface by the greenhouse effect. Greenhouse gases include carbon dioxide, water vapor, methane, chlorofluorocarbons (CFCs), ozone, and oxides of nitrogen

groundwater   water that soaks through soils and rocks, as opposed to water derived from precipitation

habitat   the home or dwelling place of an organism, such as a pine forest or a pond. Where the living place is very small, such as beneath a stone, the term *microhabitat* can be used

habitat structure   the architecture of vegetation in a habitat. The height and branching patterns of plants contribute to the complexity of vegetation architecture, and this complexity creates microhabitats for animal life

halophyte   a plant that is adapted to life in saline conditions as a result of its physical form, its physiology, or both

hydraulic conductivity a measure of the ease with which water moves through a material. Water moves easily through a material with high hydraulic conductivity

hydrology the study of the movement of water in its cycles through ecosystems and around the planet

insectivorous describing an organism that feeds upon insects and other invertebrates. The term most frequently describes predatory animals, but it may also be applied to certain plants that trap insects and digest them as a source of energy and nutrient elements

interception a function of plants in which the plant canopy catches rainwater and prevents it from reaching the ground directly. Intercepted water may continue on its way to the ground by stemflow or throughflow, or it may be evaporated back into the atmosphere

ion a charged element or group of elements. *See also* ANION and CATION

kettle hole a hollow in glacial detritus deposits resulting from the melting of a block of ice in that position. It may become filled with water to form a deep, steep-sided lake

lagg the area of fen and carr that surrounds a raised bog as groundwater flows around the edge of the peat dome

leaching the process by which ions are lost from soils and sediments as water (particularly acidic water) passes through them

lignite a soft, brown material that is intermediate between peat and bituminous coal in its stage of development

limestone sedimentary rock containing a high proportion of calcium carbonate (lime)

limnic sediments deposits formed by sedimentation in water bodies. They are commonly rich in mineral, inorganic materials derived from watershed erosion

litter the accumulation of dead (mainly plant) organic material on the surface of a soil

lycopsids a group of plants related to modern horsetails (genus *Equisetum*) that once included large wetland species that dominated the coal-forming swamps of Carboniferous times

macrofossils fossils that are large enough to be examined without the use of a microscope; sometimes referred to as megafossils

macrophyte large aquatic plant that can be observed without the use of a microscope

management in wetland ecology, the process of human manipulation of a site in order to achieve a particular end, such as by flooding, mowing, burning, or harvesting

mangal describing forested coastal ecosystems in the Tropics. The mangrove trees that form this ecosystem characteristically have upwardly bending roots that extend above the water level and act as respiratory organs

mangrove a tree or bush that grows in brackish water (diluted seawater) in the Tropics and subtropics and uses the air-exposed portion of its roots for gas exchange; also the habitat formed by these plants

marsh in American usage, a wetland with a high water level (generally above the peat or sediment surface) and dominated by herbs, usually reeds, sedges, or cattails; in European usage, a terrestrial wetland upon moist mineral soils, often maintained in a short-turf herbaceous condition by grazing and trampling. This term can cause confusion because of its two, regionally different, senses

Mediterranean climate a climate characterized by hot, dry summers and mild, moist winters. It is found in the Mediterranean basin, California, Chile, South Africa, and southwestern Australia

megafossils *see* MACROFOSSILS

methanogenic bacteria bacteria that produce methane gas as a result of their metabolism

microbes microscopic organisms such as bacteria, fungi, and viruses

microclimate the small-scale climate within habitats, such as beneath forest canopies or in the shade of rocks. The microclimate is strongly affected by habitat structure

microfossils fossils that can be observed only with the aid of a microscope, such as pollen grains, diatom frustules, and plankton remains

migration the seasonal movements of animal populations, such as geese, caribou, or even plankton moving up and down in a lake

mire a general term for any peat-forming wetland ecosystem

mire complex a wetland that consists of a series of different mire types

niche the role that a species plays in an ecosystem. The concept of niche consists of both where the species lives and how it makes its living (such its as feeding requirements, growth patterns, or reproductive behavior). The niche may be regarded as fundamental or realized

nutrient cycle the cyclic pattern of element movements between different parts of an ecosystem, together with the balance of input to and output from the ecosystem

occult precipitation precipitation that is not registered by a standard rain gauge because it arrives as mist, condensing on surfaces, including vegetation canopies. *See also* INTERCEPTION

ombrotrophic fed by rainfall. Bogs are ombrotrophic mires, receiving their water and nutrient input solely from atmospheric precipitation

oxbow lake a crescent-shaped body of water produced from an old river channel as a result of a new route being cut, concluding with the isolation of the old channel

oxidation a chemical reaction in which either oxygen is added to a material or hydrogen is taken away. Burning and respiration are familiar oxidation processes

paleoecology the study of the ecology of past communities using a variety of chemical and biological techniques

palsa a wetland type found only within the Arctic Circle. Elevated peat masses expand as a result of the development of frozen cores within them. They pass through a cycle of growth and then collapse, forming open pools

paludification a process in which an ecosystem becomes inundated with water

peat organic accumulations in wetlands resulting from the incomplete decomposition of vegetation litter

peat extraction human harvesting of peat for either energy production or horticultural applications

peat profile the cross section of a peat deposit that provides an opportunity for the study of peat stratigraphy and hence the reconstruction of past plant communities

permafrost permanently frozen subsoil. The upper layer (active layer) thaws during the summer and freezes in winter

pH an index of acidity and alkalinity. Low pH means high concentrations of hydrogen ions (hence acidity) while a high pH indicates strong alkalinity. A pH of 7 indicates neutrality. The pH scale is logarithmic, which means that, for instance, a pH of 4 is ten times as acidic as pH 5

photosynthesis the process by which certain organisms trap the energy of sunlight using a colored pigment (usually chlorophyll) and use that energy to take carbon dioxide from the atmosphere and convert it into organic molecules, initially sugars

photosynthetic bacteria bacteria possessing pigments enabling them to trap light energy and conduct photosynthesis. Some types are green and others purple in color

physiological drought a condition where water is present in a habitat but is unavailable to a plant, for instance because it is frozen

phytoplankton the collection of microscopic, often one-celled photosynthetic organisms that live in the well-lit surface layers of water bodies. They form the basis of many aquatic food webs

pioneer a species that is an initial colonist in a developing habitat

pneumatophore root structures on mangrove trees that project above the mud and act as a means of gaseous exchange with the atmosphere. They are needed because the anaerobic conditions in waterlogged mud prevent roots from respiring

pollen analysis the identification and counting of fossil pollen grains and spores stratified in peat deposits and lake sediments

pollen grains cells containing the male genetic information of flowering plants and conifers. The outer coat is robust and survives well in wetland sediments. The distinctive structure and sculpturing of the coats permit their identification even in a fossil form

polygon mire patterned wetlands of the Arctic regions, particularly apparent from the air, in which raised polygonal sections are separated by water-filled channels

population a collection of individuals of a particular species

pothole mires an extensive series of scattered wetlands found in the temperate continental regions. The North American pothole mires are important duck breeding areas

precipitation aerial deposition of water as rain, dew, snow, or in an occult form

primary productivity the rate at which new organic matter is added to an ecosystem, usually as a result of green plant photosynthesis

quaking bog a wetland in which floating vegetation extends over a lake basin from the edges, eventually forming a complete cover. The acidic, floating surface may then develop tree cover. It gets its name because it quakes when walked upon; also called Schwingmoor

raised bog   a mire in which peat accumulates to form a central dome that raises the peat-forming vegetation above the influence of groundwater flow. The surface of the central dome thus receives all its water input from precipitation (it is ombrotrophic)

rand   the sloping periphery of a raised bog

realized niche   the actual spatial and functional role of a species under competition from other species in an ecosystem. *See also* FUNDAMENTAL NICHE

reclamation   the conversion of a habitat to a condition appropriate for such human activity as agriculture or forestry

reed bed   a wetland dominated by a single species, the reed (*Phragmites australis*). The term *reed bed* is sometimes used more loosely to refer to any tall, herb-dominated marsh vegetation

rehabilitation   the conversion of a damaged ecosystem back to its original condition

relict   a species or a population left behind following the fragmentation and loss of a previously extensive range

replaceability   the ease with which a particular habitat could be replaced if it were to be lost

representativeness   the degree to which a site illustrates the major features characteristic of its habitat type

respiration   the release of energy from organic food materials by a process of controlled oxidation within the cell. Under aerobic conditions carbon dioxide is released, while anaerobic respiration may lead to the production of ethyl alcohol

rheotrophic   describing a wetland that receives its nutrient elements from both groundwater flow and precipitation. In rheotrophic mires the groundwater flow is usually responsible for the bulk of the nutrient input

rhizopods   microscopic organisms resembling *Amoeba*, but with a protective shell around their one-celled bodies. These shells are often preserved as fossils within peat deposits

salinization   accumulation of salts. Salinization is a consequence of the evaporation of water, which leaves behind the salts originally dissolved in incoming water. The wetlands of hot dry regions become saline when they have no exit drainage

salt marsh   coastal intertidal wetlands dominated by herbaceous plants

Schwingmoor   *see* QUAKING BOG

sediment   material that accumulates by sinking or being deposited over the course of time, as, for example, in a lake or a peat land. Sediments may be organic and/or mineral in their nature

sedimentation   the process of sediment accumulation

soligenous   describing mires that receive water input from groundwater sources, often fed by spring lines. Such mires are rheotrophic (flow-fed) and are usually rich in mineral nutrients

Sphagnum   *see* BOG MOSSES

spore   the one-celled dispersal structure of algae, mosses, liverworts, ferns, and fungi, from which a new individual can grow

spring mire   a peat-forming wetland that develops over springs, often having layers of mineral sediments within its profile as a consequence of water injection under pressure

stemflow   the drainage of intercepted rainwater from a plant canopy down its stem or trunk, eventually reaching the ground. *See also* THROUGHFLOW

stomata (singular: stoma)   tiny pores through which leaf surfaces take in the gas carbon dioxide from the atmosphere as they photosynthesize and lose water in the process of transpiration

stratification   the layering of lake sediments and peats in the chronological order of their accumulation

stratigraphy   the study of layering in sediments and the description of sediment profiles. Stratigraphy can provide information on the developmental sequence of a mire over time

stratosphere   the part of the Earth's atmosphere lying above the troposphere, from around nine to 30 miles (15 to 50 km)

strings   the raised ridges running along the contours of aapa mires (string bogs). The linear pools between them are termed flarks

string bog   *see* AAPA MIRE

stromatolite   rocklike mounds formed by cyanobacteria in shallow seas. They are found fossil dating as far back as Precambrian times

submerged aquatic plants   freshwater macrophytes (plants large enough to be visible to the naked eye) that are rooted in soil that lies underwater and grow toward but not above the water surface, although some carry flowers that extend above the water surface. *See also* EMERGENT AQUATIC PLANTS

succession   the process of ecosystem development, which is driven by the immigration of new species, facilitation by environmental alteration, competitive struggles, and eventually some degree of equilibration at the climax stage. The stages of succession often follow a predictable sequence. The process usually involves an increase in the biomass of the ecosystem, although the development of raised bog from carr is an exception to this

sulfide zone   the waterlogged, anaerobic catotelm in a peat profile. It is so named because a silver wire inserted into this zone in the peat profile becomes rapidly blackened by silver sulfide

swamp   a vegetated wetland in which the summer water level remains above the sediment surface so that there is always a covering of water. In North America, the term is restricted to forested wetlands of this kind, while in Europe the term is normally used only of herbaceous reed beds and cattail marshes

tephra   the glasslike dust particles emitted from erupting volcanoes. Layers of tephra in peat stratigraphy can serve as time markers, since the dates of eruptions are well known and the chemistry of tephra often indicates the precise volcanic eruption involved

terrestrial   occurring on land

terrestrialization   the process of succession whereby aquatic ecosystems gradually fill in with sediment

terrestric sediments   materials that are deposited above the prevailing water table, such as the peats of raised bogs

throughflow   the dripping of intercepted rainwater through a plant canopy to reach the ground. *See also* STEM-FLOW

topogenous   describing a mire that receives water by runoff from surrounding slopes. Such mires are flow-fed (rheotrophic)

transpiration   the loss of water vapor from the leaves of terrestrial plants through the stomata, or pores, in the leaf surface

troposphere   the lower layer of the Earth's atmosphere, up to about nine miles (15 km)

tundra   the open vegetation of cold, Arctic conditions. Trees are absent, apart from dwarf species of willow and birch

valley mire   strictly a mire complex, consisting of a central stream and surrounding fen or carr vegetation, and lateral poor fens in which the flow of water is slow and the nutrient supply is restricted. Although often called a "valley bog" because of the acidity and nutrient poverty of the lateral regions, the wetland normally remains rheotrophic (flow-fed), so is not a true bog (which is rain-fed, or ombrotrophic)

vulnerability   the degree to which an ecosystem is threatened with conversion to alternate uses, such as drainage of a wetland for use in agriculture or forestry. *See also* FRAGILITY

water level   the height at which water stands above the sediment surface in a wetland

watershed   the geographical region from which water drains into a particular stream or wetland (equivalent to catchment). The term is also used to describe the ridge separating two catchments—literally the region where water may be shed in either of two directions

water table   the level at which water is maintained in the soil within the ecosystem

wetland   a general term covering all shallow aquatic ecosystems (freshwater and marine) together with marshes, swamps, fens, and bogs

xeromorphic   structurally adapted to resist drought

zonation   the banding of vegetation along an environmental gradient, as in the transition around a shallow water body from submerged and floating aquatic plants, emergent aquatics, then to reed bed, and finally swamp

BIBLIOGRAPHY AND FURTHER READING

General biogeography

Archibold, O. W. *Ecology of World Vegetation.* New York: Chapman & Hall, 1995.

Bradbury, Ian K. *The Biosphere.* New York: Wiley, 2nd ed., 1998.

Brown, J. H., and M. V. Lomolino. *Biogeography.* Sunderland, Mass.: Sinauer Associates, 2nd ed., 1998.

Cox, C. B., and P. D. Moore. *Biogeography: An Ecological and Evolutionary Approach.* Oxford: Blackwell Publishing, 7th ed., 2005.

Gaston, K. J., and J. I. Spicer. *Biodiversity: An Introduction.* Oxford: Blackwell Publishing, 2nd ed., 2004.

General wetlands

Charman, D. *Peatlands and Environmental Change.* New York: Wiley, 2002.

Gore, A. J. P., ed. *Ecosystems of the World—Mires: Swamp, Bog, Fen and Moor.* 2 vols. Amsterdam: Elsevier, 1983.

Moore, P. D. *Wetlands.* New York: Facts On File, 2001.

Williams, Michael, ed. *Wetlands: A Threatened Landscape.* Oxford: Blackwell Publishing, 1990.

Wetland conservation

Houghton, J. *Global Warming: The Complete Briefing.* Cambridge: Cambridge University Press, 3rd ed., 2004.

Maltby, Edward. *Waterlogged Wealth.* Washington, D.C.: Earthscan, 1986.

Parkyn, L., R. E. Stoneman, and H. A. P. Ingram, eds. *Conserving Peatlands.* Wallingford, U.K.: CABI, 1997.

Wheeler, Bryan D., Susan C. Shaw, Wanda J. Fojt, and R. Allan Robertson, eds. *Restoration of Temperate Wetlands.* New York: Wiley, 1995.

Wetland history and development

Brothwell, Don. *The Bog Man and the Archaeology of People.* London: British Museum Publications, 1986.

Coles, B., and J. Coles. *People of the Wetlands: Bogs, Bodies, and Lake Dwellers.* London: Guild Publishing, 1989.

Delcourt, P. A., and H. R. Delcourt. *Prehistoric Native Americans and Ecological Change.* Cambridge: Cambridge University Press, 2004.

Godwin, Sir Harry. *Fenland: Its Ancient Past and Uncertain Future.* Cambridge: Cambridge University Press, 1978.

———. *The Archives of the Peat Bogs.* Cambridge: Cambridge University Press, 1981.

Moore, P. D., J. A. Webb, and M. E. Collinson. *Pollen Analysis.* Oxford: Blackwell Science, 2nd ed., 1991.

Prince, Hugh. *Wetlands of the American Midwest: A Historical Geography of Changing Attitudes.* Chicago: University of Chicago Press, 1997.

Whitney, Gordon G. *From Coastal Wilderness to Fruited Plain: A History of Environmental Change in Temperate North America from 1500 to the Present.* Cambridge: Cambridge University Press, 1994.

The wetland ecosystem and its inhabitants

Araujo-Lima, Carlos, and Michael Goulding. *So Fruitful a Fish: Ecology, Conservation and Aquaculture of the Amazon's Tambaqui.* New York: Columbia University Press, 1997.

Ashman, M. R., and G. Puri. *Essential Soil Science.* Oxford: Blackwell Science, 2002.

Crawford, R. M. M., ed. *Plant Life in Aquatic and Amphibious Habitats.* Oxford: Blackwell Science, 1987.

Rheinheimer, G. *Aquatic Microbiology.* New York: Wiley, 4th ed., 1991.

Westlake, D. F., J. Kvet, and A. Szczepanski, eds. *The Production Ecology of Wetlands.* Cambridge: Cambridge University Press, 1998.

North American wetlands

Davis, Steven M., and John C. Ogden, eds. *Everglades: The Ecosystem and Its Restoration.* Delray Beach, Fla.: St. Lucie Press, 1994.

Martin, William H., Stephen G. Boyce, and Arthur C. Echternacht, eds. *Biodiversity of the Southeastern United States: Lowland Terrestrial Communities.* New York: Wiley, 1993.

Myers, Ronald L., and John J. Ewel, eds. *Ecosystems of Florida.* Orlando: University of Central Florida Press, 1990.

Schoenherr, Allan A. *A Natural History of California.* Berkeley: University of California Press, 1992.

World wetlands

Allanson, B. R., and D. Baird, eds. *Estuaries of South Africa*. Cambridge: Cambridge University Press, 1999.

Forrester, Bob, Mike Murray-Hudson, and Lance Cherry. *The Swamp Book: A View of the Okavango*. Johannesburg: Southern Publishers, 1989.

Goulding, Michael, Nigel J. H. Smith, and Dennis J. Mahar. *Floods of Fortune: Ecology and Economy along the Amazon*. New York: Columbia University Press, 1996.

Knystautas, Algirdas. *The Natural History of the U.S.S.R.* London: Century, 1987.

Moore, Peter D., ed. *European Mires*. New York: Academic Press, 1984.

Rieley, J. O., and S. E. Page, eds. *Biodiversity and Sustainability of Tropical Peatlands*. Cardigan, U.K.: Samara Publishing, 1997.

Tomlinson, P. B. *The Botany of Mangroves*. Cambridge: Cambridge University Press, 1986.

WEB SITES

Conservation International

URL: http://www.conservation.org

Particularly concerned with global biological conservation.

Earthwatch Institute

URL: http://www.earthwatch.org

General environmental problems worldwide.

International Union for the Conservation of Nature

URL: http://www.redlist.org

Many links to other sources of information on particular species, especially those currently endangered.

National Parks Service of the United States

URL: http://www.nps.gov

Information on specific conservation problems facing the National Parks.

Sierra Club

URL: http://www.sierraclub.org

Covers general conservation issues in the United States and also issues relating to farming and land use.

U.S. Fish and Wildlife Service

URL: http://www.nwi.fws.gov

A valuable resource for information on wildlife conservation.

U.S. Geological Survey

URL: http://www.usgs.gov

Covers environmental problems affecting landscape conservation.

United Nations Environmental Program World Conservation Monitoring Center

URL: http://www.unep-wcmw.org

Good for global statistics on environmental problems.

Note: *Italic* page numbers refer to illustrations.

Pizarro, Gonzalo 145–146
plankton 11. *See also*
  phytoplankton; zoo-
  plankton
plants 98–105. *See also*
  photosynthesis
  aquatic. *See* aquatic
    plants
  in Arctic wetlands 30,
    31, 32, 34
  autotrophic nutrition
    of 69
  in blanket bogs
    27–28
  carbon need of
    82–83
  carnivorous 104–105
  in coastal wetlands
    35, 36
  in fens 15
  growth of 49, 89
  invertebrates eating
    110
  microscopic. *See* phy-
    toplankton
  nitrogen need of 48,
    84, 104, 105
  pollen grains of 52,
    55, 59–62, *61*
  in pothole mires 22
  in raised bogs 24, 25,
    26, 40
  roots of 52, 89–91,
    95, 99, 101
  in sediment formation
    52
  in spring mires 17–18
  in swamps 18, *19*, 20.
    See also swamp
    forests

water abundance and
  94
and water movement
  8, 9
Plasmodium (genus) 136,
  137
pollen grains, in sedi-
  ments 52, 55, 59–62,
  61
pollution. *See also* climate
  change; environmental
  change
  and acid rain 84–85
  of wetlands 173–175.
    See also climate
    change
polygon mires 30–31, *31*
polyphenols 80
pond skaters 109
pondweeds 96
poor fens 15–16
population 68
potassium 50
pothole mires 21–22, *22*,
  158, *158*
prairie pothole mires 21,
  22, 158, *158*
precipitation. *See also*
  rain; snow
  abundance of 3, 6
  formation of 1–2, 5–6
  occult 9
  ocean currents and
    6–7
  in water cycle 2, *3*
predatory animals
  birds 121
  energy efficiency of
    77
  fish 111–112

heterotrophic nutri-
  tion of 69
invertebrates 109,
  111
mammals 124, 125
prehistoric people xviii,
  129–134
primates 126
productivity, of wetlands
  76–77, 79–80
protein 48, 104
protists 107. *See also*
  fungi; phytoplankton;
  zooplankton
pyramid of biomass 78–79
python, Indian 115

Q

quaking bogs 22–23, *23*
quinine 136

R

radiocarbon analysis 63
rail 119
rain
  acidity of 42, 46,
    84–85, 174, 175
  canopy interception
    of 8, 9
  climate change and
    176–177
  formation of 1, 2, 5–6
  movement of, in val-
    ley 7–10, *8*
  in temperate regions
    6
  in Tropics 5
  wetlands fed by. *See*
    ombrotrophic wet-
    lands